# LAST MINUTE COVER LETTERS

By
BRANDON TOROPOV

CAREER PRESS
3 Tice Road, P.O. Box 687
Franklin Lakes, NJ 07417
1-800-CAREER-1; 201-848-0310 (NJ and outside U.S.)
FAX: 201-848-1727

LAST MINUTE COVER LETTERS

Cover design by Foster & Foster

Printed in the U.S.A. by Book-mart Press

To order this title, please call toll-free 1-800-CAREER-1 (NJ and Canada: 201-848-0310) to order using VISA or MasterCard, or for further information on books from Career Press.

## Library of Congress Cataloging-in-Publication Data

Toropov, Brandon.
    Last minute cover letters / by Brandon Toropov.
        p.    cm.
    ISBN 1-56414-353-8 (pbk.)
    1. Cover letters.    I. Title.
HF5383.T666      1998
808'.06665--dc21                                          98-19375

*To*
*Stephen*

# Acknowledgments

Ron Fry showed his usual faith, vision, and patience in helping me turn this book from idea into actuality. The following superior firms made contributions to this volume: Executive Resume, (Cedar Brook, New Jersey); S&A Business Services, (Bloomfield, Missouri); Resume Center of New York, (College Point, New York); Resumes by James, (Forest Hills, New York); WSA Corporation, (Shawnee, Kansas). For contact information on all of these firms see the Appendix.

# CONTENTS

Introduction                                                                    9

## PART I: LAST MINUTE COVER LETTERS

Chapter 1

Opportunity Alert! Landing a Job in Little Time                                13

Chapter 2

Researching a Last-Minute Opening Within Your Company                          17

Chapter 3

Researching Last-Minute Opportunities at New Companies                         21

Chapter 4

Creating an Effective Talent Match Letter                                      25

Chapter 5

Success Stories to Make Your Cover Letter a Standout                           29

Chapter 6

Developing a Door-Opening Resume Package                                       33

Chapter 7

    Mailing Your Package for Maximum Effect      43

Chapter 8

    Some Thoughts on Rejection: Turning Lemons into Lemonade      51

Chapter 9

    10 Final Words to the Wise      55

## PART II: SAMPLE COVER LETTERS

    Powerful, dramatic, concise cover letters written      59
        for applicants in a variety of fields

Appendix      151

Index      155

# Introduction

Who says you can't get a great job in a hurry?

This book assumes you can. It includes dozens of superior cover letter templates you can use right now to make your application shine...even if you don't have a lot of time on your hands. It also offers some important advice that will help you make the most of the time you have to put together a great cover letter, stand out from the crowd, and get the interview and the job offer you deserve.

Here's what you can expect in the way of advice, guidance, and valuable tips in the first part of *Last Minute Cover Letters:*

- In Chapter 1, you learn why research is important in developing your cover letter (and other written materials), even if you're short on time.

- In Chapter 2, you find out how to find out more about an opening at the organization where you're already working.

- In Chapter 3, you learn how to conduct an instant research campaign on openings at a firm with which you're unfamiliar.

- In Chapter 4, you learn about composing a Talent Match letter—a valuable precursor to both resume and cover letter—that may help you distinguish yourself from the pack.

- In Chapter 5, you learn how to develop success stories that will help you add drama and immediate appeal to your cover letters.

- In Chapter 6, you learn how to put together a door-opening resume package.

- In Chapter 7, you find out what to send when—and how to maximize your chances of landing the interview.

- Feeling dejected about your last call? Don't. In Chapter 8, you learn why even a "no" answer doesn't have to mean the end of the trail for you.

- In Chapter 9, you learn about 10 things you really *shouldn't* do when you're short on time and you have to set up a superior cover letter.

Then there's the main attraction: In the second part of the book, you get a wealth of sample cover letters, many of them written by some of the most accomplished career experts in the land. After that, you get a couple of valuable bonus sections—special letters for before and after your interview, and referrals to some of the best employment professionals in the country.

That's a lot of ground to cover—so let's get going!

# PART I

## LAST MINUTE
## COVER LETTERS

# CHAPTER 1

# Opportunity Alert! Landing a Job in Little Time

*"Sleep faster—we need the pillows."*

—Yiddish proverb

It's time to take action. You need to develop a superior cover letter—fast.

Why? There could be any number of reasons: Maybe your own job-search calls have led you to an opportunity that you want to act on quickly. Maybe you've seen a job listing within your own company—one you know won't stay open for long. Maybe you're responding to a soon-to-be public job-search listing that hasn't been advertised yet, and you know that time is of the essence. Maybe a friend from another company called to tell you of a sudden opening. Maybe your finances have dwindled after a long job hunt, and you want to develop a letter that will help you land a new job as soon as possible. Whichever situation you find yourself in, this book will help.

It's great to have obtained a referral for a choice position—but sometimes you won't have this advantage. In this early part of the book, we'll look at the scenarios—when you have the inside track, and when you don't. You'll find out the best ways for you to craft a targeted last-minute cover letter that's right for your situation. And you'll also learn how to take full advantage of the opportunities that present themselves. After you have reviewed the advice that appears in the first half of this book, you'll want to turn to the second half of the book, which offers a wide variety of sample cover letters for you to use as models.

# Research counts!

The importance of developing *some* research for your target organization can't be overemphasized. Most of your competitors for this position will, in all likelihood, fail to do even minimal amounts of research on the opportunity for which they're applying. Even though you're short on time, you owe it to yourself to develop a letter that appeals directly to the concerns of greatest interest to the hiring official at your target company. The more you know about the company you're sending material to, the more likely your appeal will be successful.

You must be ready to be specific about how you would fit in at the firm where you are hoping to work. This means that you need to do a little bit of research on yourself, as well as on the company you're contacting. How will *you* add value to your prospective employer?

To answer that question, you need to have a strong sense of "mission"—of where you're going and why it makes sense for you to go there. In other words, you have to develop a good idea of the kind of contribution you can realistically see yourself making. This is an important point, because employers are often just as impressed with an applicant's firm sense of purpose as they are with any narrow element of his or her record of experience. Knowing what you want to do—and how it will benefit the prospective employer—is an essential prerequisite for success on the job-search front. If you hope to get a job quickly, you'll want to be able to talk about what you want to do—and how your prospective employer will benefit from what you do.

Get a fix on what you do best—and what you *like* to do most—that will add value to a company. Think back to your greatest successes in life, those on the job and outside of work, as well. For example, did you coach a youth soccer team? Write and edit the PTA newsletter? Chair a successful fund-raising effort for a community organization? Don't discount such achievements and activities just because you don't get paid for them. As you consider all of your contributions and skills, include experiences from both the volunteer world and your on-the-job history for the past five to 10 years, and ask yourself these questions:

- What are/were my main responsibilities in each situation?
- What skills do/did I bring to each of these ventures?
- What new skills did I develop in each case?
- What successes, achievements, and positive results did I accomplish for each of these situations?
- What three projects or achievements am I proudest of? Why?
- What promotions, raises, awards, or commendations have I received?
- What do/did superiors comment on about my work?
- How do/did I work with other people? Supervisors? Co-workers? Employees?

Of course, if you're trying to land a job fast, you don't have time for a lengthy, soul-searching journey. But it's important to know yourself—your skills, successes, and strengths—and as much about the job opportunity you're pursuing as possible. This will enable you to best position yourself as the best person for that position—from your first contact through your cover letter and resume package all the way to your final interview.

You will get much better results by saying, "My aim is to be a technical writing specialist at a Fortune 100 company in the New York City metropolitan area," than you will by saying, "I can do anything." A great many unsuccessful cover letters suffer from the "I can do anything" syndrome: They make employers connect the dots when it comes to figuring out how past experience is likely to translate to future contributions.

To develop a goal that makes sense to both you and the prospective employer, then, you'll need to find out a little more about the organization behind that time-sensitive opportunity you've just learned about. It's time to look in detail at the best ways to research the firm you're targeting in the (limited) time available to you.

CHAPTER 2

# Researching a Last-Minute Opening Within Your Company

*"He who refuses to embrace a unique opportunity loses the prize as surely as if he had tried and failed."*
—William James, 19th-century American philosopher

Because you're "in the loop" at your company, you're in an excellent position to be considered for opportunities that open up within your firm. First, you're likely to learn about these openings sooner than job-seekers outside the firm. Secondly, you're in a position to know more about the opening. And, finally, the company knows more about you and your terrific qualifications and skills.

Still, just because you have an advantage doesn't mean you can sit back and wait for the offer. Chances are there are others within the company who are vying for the same opening. So get to work!

Let's assume that you only have a few days in which to apply for this position—either because of formal applications restrictions or because you know the competition will be intense—and let's assume that you haven't applied for a job with this person in the past. How can you make the most of the time at hand?

During the next few precious days, you will want to find a way to get your candidacy to show up on the hiring supervisor's radar screen. You want to become a priority on the overcrowded desk, and make it onto the person's to-do list. In order to do this, you will first need to know the qualifications of the position you are seeking. The more clearly you understand the demands of the position, the skills and education needed, the better you will be able to match your strengths with the existing job qualifications—and communicate them. You have an advantage; because you are looking within your own organization, it should be relatively easy to obtain a formal job description, or to locate someone who can give you an informal description. Are there formal job postings or summaries of responsibilities that you can review? Other individuals within your company who've held this job in the past? Completed projects you can review? All of these will be helpful as you craft your letter and plan your strategy.

# The person to meet

The last person who recently held the position, or who is preparing to leave it, holds a wealth of information about the job. It's usually a good idea to try to locate this person and initiate a conversation about the pros and cons of the job. Although it's easy to trade information at the water cooler, it might be better to talk off-site; consider extending a lunch invitation. Here both of you can speak freely and you might obtain some insights into the position—its benefits as well as its pitfalls—that you might not otherwise know.

You are going to get some hints that might assist you in getting on the inside track. It might be helpful, for instance, to find out what kind of person your prospective new boss is—about his or her likes, dislikes, hobbies, and work habits. This is also a prime opportunity to find out what the position's main responsibilities are—what challenges it poses, what skills are required. Talk with someone who's held the job in the past to help you augment your existing knowledge about the job. Find out:

- What are the supervisor's most important goals for this position?
- What are the skills required—and do they differ from those you might expect?
- What educational background is required?
- What is the best part of working for this person?
- What are the greatest challenges?
- What does the average workday look like?
- What are the most pressing current issues?
- How much interaction with outside contacts—vendors, clients, and the like—will be required?
- What internal relationships are likely to be most important?
- Is travel a part of the job?

The insights you gain will help you to present your strengths in the best possible light. Even if you have some idea about the dimensions of this position already, or have heard office gossip, it doesn't hurt to confirm what you've heard. But don't start spreading tales of your own! You want to use all the advantages that come with applying for an inside position, while avoiding the possible pitfalls. One of those pitfalls is getting distracted by the rumor mill. Gather the data you need, but don't spread stories—or even assume that everything you hear is gospel.

With new information, you may find yourself more—or less— interested in the job. But more than likely, you will uncover critical information that will allow you to save yourself a costly mistake when you apply for the job. For instance, if you learn that your potential new manager is eager to find help in developing written proposals to win new business, you'll want to highlight skills in that area—even if that requirement isn't listed on the formal job description.

# Beware of ruffling feathers

Be cautious when exploring employment opportunities within your current company. Careful consideration of the culture in which you are working, and an awareness of any political issues affecting your office and the one you are planning to apply to, are vital. If you feel that your current supervisor could be threatened by your move, you may want to keep high-profile personal contacts to a minimum— or you may even decide that limiting your appeals to written form makes the most sense for you. This may mean building your cover letter around your current understanding of the job requirements. There is a possibility that by applying for this new position you may jeopardize your current job, or at least make it less enjoyable! You may want to consider taking a low-key approach to the job search.

Once you have developed information about the opening, you will want to build a powerful cover letter, one that matches the job description as closely as possible. Ideally—whether you're applying "from the inside" or "from the outside"—your letter should focus closely and concisely on the ways *you* fulfill key requirements for the job.

Having completed some internal research, you're ready to move forward with your candidacy. You can begin to focus your efforts on building an impressive Talent Match letter—a powerful piece of correspondence that may precede a resume package—or on developing a standard cover letter to accompany your resume. Both documents are discussed in detail a little later in this book.

But first—suppose the last-minute opening you're interested in *isn't* at the company that's employing you now? How do you make the most of the time available to you in that situation? You'll find the answer to that question in the next chapter.

# CHAPTER 3

# Researching Last-Minute Opportunities at New Companies

*"I'm not the kind of guy to knock at a door and then when the door is opened not go in."*
—William Saroyan, 20th-century American writer

When you have no "insider" contacts at an organization, you're forced to consider alternative strategies. After all, you don't know a co-worker who can point you toward key considerations about company objectives, competition, and products and services. There is no colleague who can save you research time, and your own knowledge of the company in question is likely to be limited. With only a few days to act, you need to find out as much as you can about the target company, so that you can aim your written and oral messages specifically to the needs of the company and job position. What do you do when you have to get the best possible information on a company—and a job opening—in a very short period of time?

# Four steps to information-gathering

The following four steps can help you find out more about the opening for which you're applying. In most cases, you'll be able to complete all four in a single day.

*Step 1. Ask for a written copy of the job description.* Whether it comes from the personnel office or from someone else, you'll want to review all the particulars. If you can, have the information faxed or e-mailed to you directly. There's no point in waiting two to three days when time is of the essence.

*Step 2. Ask whether the company has a Web site—if it does, fire up your browser.* Approximately 50 percent of all small businesses and a much larger percentage of larger companies have a World Wide Web presence today. In a matter of minutes you can take a look at a prospective employer's Web site and gather all kinds of information on its development, its principals, and the kind of business it does. The Web site may also offer an employment page with information and current openings and job descriptions.

If you're uneasy about your computer skills, get a friend to do a quick search for you (and make a commitment to upgrade your level of computer literacy in the very near future—employers tend to notice this sort of skill gap these days).

*Step 3. Call the hiring manager or other key official.* If you don't know who the hiring manager is, calling the president's office is often a great way to gather further information. If you are seeking a management position, this may be helpful in demonstrating initiative and interest. It may gain you some valuable insights on directions and changes within the company that have not yet been posted on the Web or appeared in publication.

One of the secrets that great networkers know is that the president's assistant can be a source of vital information, and probably the gatekeeper to the powers of the company. When you call and speak to the administrative assistant, it is important to make a professional impression. Have a carefully prepared list of questions such as: What new directions is the company taking in the upcoming year, or quarter? What new products is it releasing? If you are unable to reach the president, the assistant may be a great source of information about organizational issues, mission statements—and questions about which key projects are underway at any given moment and how you might be able to help contribute to those. This person also has a finger on the pulse of the political environment and the power players.

*Step 4. Hit the library.* The local library is a great place to gather information about prospective employers. Plan to spend an entire day tracking down information on the company—it's time wisely spent! Most libraries have a text search retrieval computer. This service will allow you to punch in the name of the company or perhaps even the industry, a key product or service, and pull up any articles that have been published in the last six months in major newspapers or magazines. You'll want to take the time to at least skim all of the recent articles. While you are at the library, take advantage of the time to look at the business section of periodicals. Current economic trends, particularly those that will affect the industry and company you are hoping to work for may give you valuable insights.

The reference librarian can be a great help, and can probably assist you in tracking down some of the company's annual reports. If the library doesn't have the company's annual reports, the reference librarian may be able to point you toward a business branch of a larger library. If the target company is publicly held, it issues an annual report that specifically points out where the company has been, where it's going, and what it's financial performance is. The report may also have some important information about new products, mission statements, and other information.

Don't overlook trade magazines and business newspapers that cover the industry of your target company—or the industry sectors it serves. You'll want to look at several recent issues. Obviously you're looking for references to your target company, but you're also looking to find out about the most recent trends in the industry. Similarly, you may want to review such newspapers as *The Wall Street Journal* (which is comparatively easy and interesting to read).

You may be tempted to skip the trade magazines. Written for insiders, their text is often highly technical. They may look glitzy from the outside, but they are written for knowledgeable insiders and it is often difficult for others to understand the technical jargon they use. Remember: Your goal is to *become* an insider, to be knowledgeable in the field in which you'll be making contributions. It is important for you to be able to speak with at least some knowledge of current industry trends. Take time at the library to review the most recent issues of the magazine or newspaper that decision-makers in your target industry will be reading.

At the end of this full (but exhausting!) day, you will have successfully tracked down a great deal of helpful information on the target company and the industry in which it operates. Add this research to the job description you've tracked down, and you can begin putting together your Talent Match letter! Let's move on to the next chapter.

# CHAPTER 4

# Creating an Effective Talent Match Letter

*"Enthusiasm finds the opportunities, and energy makes the most of them."*

—Henry S. Haskins, 20th-century American writer

Consider this before you submit your application for any job opening: The employer may have received more than 100 replies to an advertised job. With a desk strewn with papers, your contact person can't possibly read every line of every piece of job-related correspondence that has come in. That individual is seeking shortcuts—trying to weed out the least promising candidates and focus only on the most promising ones. Your objective, of course, is to make the cut.

You are trying to gain notice and attention, to move from the larger pile of "everyone" into the smaller pile of "possible candidates." The best method for moving into the "choice" group, I believe, is to use a Talent Match letter. Derivations of this effective tool have been recommended by savvy career counselors for several years now—but few job-seekers take advantage of it. You may not *always* be able to use this specialized letter—sometimes the target organization or the demands of the situation you face will dictate another approach—but you will want to learn how to assemble it in order to take advantage of those situations in which it's likely to be of greatest benefit to you.

# What is a Talent Match letter?

This is a letter sent (or hand-delivered) in place of a traditional resume/cover letter package. The Talent Match letter serves to introduce you to a company in the most positive way possible, while eliminating any—repeat *any*—reasons *not* to interview you for the position in question. It's concise; it's direct; it's relentlessly upbeat.

In order to create a Talent Match letter, you need to track down the formal requirements of the position, using the methods discussed in previous chapters. You will want to examine carefully the best information you have on the position's requirements by consulting a job description, your notes from discussions with key people, or other formal or informal sources.

You may, for example, find out that the position of publishing assistant has three key requirements:

- Three years of experience with Microsoft Word.
- Two years of experience in electronic publishing.
- One year of exposure to advertising sales.

On your Talent Match letter you would then set up two columns: "Requirements for Publishing Assistant" and "My Skills." Above the columns you will write a brief statement introducing yourself. The example on the following page shows what the Talent Match letter might look like in practice.

Jane Smith
123 Main Street
Boston, MA 01949
(617) 555-5555

December 7, 1998

Mr. Leo Gonzales
Vice President, Personnel
Freeway Publishing
1117 Fourth Avenue
Boston, MA 02139

Dear Mr. Gonzalez:

Thanks for taking the time to talk to me today over the phone. Here is why I believe you and I should meet to discuss the possibility of my becoming the new publishing assistant for ABC Corporation:

| Requirements for Publishing Assistant | Jane Smith's Skills |
| --- | --- |
| 3 years of experience with MS Word | 5 years of experience with MS Word |
| 2 years of experience in electronic publishing | 2 years of experience in electronic publishing |
| 1 year of exposure to advertising sales | 2 years of exposure to advertising sales |

I'll be looking forward to speaking with you when I call Monday morning, December 14. If you have any questions in the meantime, please don't hesitate to give me a call before then.

Sincerely,

Jane Smith

It's highly unlikely that this kind of letter will find its way into the proverbial "circular file." There's simply no reason to reject it!

Remember, the Talent Match letter *replaces* the traditional resume package, including cover letter. It has all the advantages of such a mailing, but also leaves you the option of passing along your (more detailed, more thoroughly researched) resume in person during a face-to-face meeting. When should you send the Talent Match letter? We'll examine that question a little later in the book.

One of the advantages of using a Talent Match letter is that it opens the door for you to call. Rather than waiting by the phone for a prospective employer to follow up with you, you get to take action. In a fair number of cases, the person you send this letter to will not only remember your correspondence, but will be awaiting your call.

It's important to call exactly as promised—and to leave a polite message in the event that you are unable to get through to the person. You might leave a poised, polite voice-mail message stating that you called and would look forward to hearing from your contact, and that you will call back on such-and-such a day if you don't hear from him or her.

The Talent Match letter should be your opening salvo in your last-minute campaign—but it won't be your only piece of ammunition. To learn about the other weapons at your disposal, read on!

# CHAPTER 5

# Success Stories to Make Your Cover Letter a Standout

*"Lucky is the man who need not search his pockets for words."*
—Russian proverb

Once you develop your Talent Match letter, you will have laid the groundwork for later work on other powerful letters that can help you set your candidacy apart in the eyes of the hiring official. A single compelling anecdote, briefly delivered in your cover letter, can make all the difference in your candidacy. But you may have to do some digging if you want to come up with that single compelling anecdote! To get the right story, you'll need to start looking in detail at what you've done right in the past.

It's time to review your own work history. Just as you have lined up your qualifications next to the job's requirements, you now want to be able to communicate your past successes in key areas. In other words, you want to convey the idea that you would be a worthy addition to the company, someone who can make an important contribution in short order.

You must be ready to convey, in both written and verbal forms, your most powerful success stories. Using condensed versions of these stories will add impact and interest to your cover letters. The right success stories aren't really that difficult to identify, and they do have a way of impressing employers.

# Three success themes

One of the areas where you'll want to develop success stories has to do with your own adaptability. You should be able to demonstrate that you are comfortable with change. In other words, in the midst of change, expected or not, you have acted positively to the benefit of your employer. Think for a moment about times when your organization has had to change its way of functioning. Is there a seasonal, monthly, or quarterly rush? Have you ever been called upon to act in a business crisis? Was the company in danger of losing a valued client when you stepped in? Perhaps you took the initiative in learning and teaching a new software program to people in your department, or stepped in for someone who was ill and performed capably at a moment's notice.

Take some time to consider the changes you were confronted with in your previous work experiences, the ability you have for dealing with change, and the positive effect your abilities have had on your organization. Start jotting down some notes and some initial ideas. Consider reviewing these with a friend or a co-worker. In today's rapidly changing, global economy, some industries change with startling speed. With fluid market conditions, new technologies, and ever-changing customer bases that have the potential to vanish overnight, the ability to work constructively through change is a valuable asset to any employer.

Another major area of success deals with profit orientation and efficiency. You show up at work to do more than just punch in and punch out. Your new employer hopes to hire someone who is dedicated, excited about the company's goals, and personally committed to seeing the company's mission carried out. It's important to develop a few good stories in this area, as well.

Think of a time when you came up with a smarter, less wasteful way to do something at work. Exactly how—in terms of hard numbers—did this benefit the firm? Did you come up with a new system for storing important records, and thereby help to increase by 15 percent the number of completed reports that your department submitted in a given quarter? Did you pass along ideas for streamlining sales presentations—ideas that contributed to your department posting a 30-percent increase in revenues? Did you help to develop new product ideas that resulted in quarterly sales growth of 100,000 units for a particular fiscal year?

The third area is "customer orientation." Whether or not you're a salesperson, you'll want to convey to your prospective employer that you understand the customer, that you are not removed from the actual application of your work. You understand how your work contributes to the end-user's experience, and you are concerned with finding ways to keep the customer satisfied.

Have you ever resolved a customer service problem creatively? Assisted in a sales presentation? Identified a "glitch" that was keeping a customer or end-user from getting your organization's best? How about "selling" new ideas internally? Was there ever a time when you advocated for a new technology solution, put a new idea across, made a proposal, or implemented change within your organization. Were you successful? And what was the response of your co-workers or boss? Write down the details. (This area is particularly important, of course, if you are applying for a sales or customer service position!)

You want to demonstrate leadership ability, as well as flexibility and creativity in dealing with internal and external challenges.

You want to convey not only that you can successfully rise to the challenge of change with quantifiable results, but that you have the sales ability needed by a leader to effectively guide and support others both inside and outside the organization.

You may find that some of your stories overlap categories and that you can use one story to articulate all three categories. Spend some time developing these success stories, both orally and in written form. Then consider which of your stories are best tied into the needs of the job description that you are currently examining. Dramatic, relevant success stories should significantly shorten your job search.

Talk to others who know you and who are in a position to coach you on your own successes. Then practice, practice, practice. Write your stories several ways, and say them several ways. Keep in mind that your goal is not only to line up your success stories with the job qualifications—but also to be able to be comfortable communicating your successes at a moment's notice.

To recap: You will want your cover letter (and, indeed, all the materials you pass along during your last-minute job search campaign) to reinforce at least one, and possibly all three, of the following messages:

- You are adaptable and deal well with change.

- You know that efficiency and bottom-line results are essential.

- You have a good sense of the organization's products and/or services, and you could, if you had to, explain what the company has to offer in a compelling way to a prospective customer.

Once you've prepared concise success stories in this area, you'll want to learn how the written components of your last-minute job search will support one another—and how you can avoid the most common cover letter mistakes. That's where the next chapter will help.

# CHAPTER 6

# Developing a Door-Opening Resume Package

*"The world is all gates, all opportunities, strings of tension waiting to be struck."*

—Ralph Waldo Emerson

What are the ground rules for developing an effective last-minute mailing campaign? In this chapter, you'll see how the various elements of your job-search mailings can and should support each other. In the next chapter, you will learn how to establish a mailing schedule that allows each of the components—including the Talent Match letter discussed in the previous chapter—to work most effectively.

First and foremost, understand that you should *never* mail a resume without a cover letter. There are three reasons for this: First, employers *expect* to see a cover letter attached to a resume. Second, the cover letter is your opportunity to communicate directly—and more personally—to the reader in a way that the more formal resume format does not. Finally, you can use your cover letter to emphasize key strengths or accomplishments that match the job description you're exploring. Although your resume may include this information, the cover letter gives you a chance to highlight it, calling it to the attention of the reader—who may skim through your resume without recognizing a very important selling point.

# Some advice about design

Your candidacy will benefit tremendously from the professional look of matching paper for your resume, cover letter, and envelopes. If it takes time for you to nail down a particular opening—and it may—you could find yourself passing along a whole series of documents: letters, resumes, preliminary proposals, names of references. You will want every sheet to match every other sheet; this will help you establish yourself as a sharp, consistent professional. Be sure to select a quality paper stock in white or ivory—stay away from bright colors, even pastels.

Today's word processors and computers make it easy to develop and to continue the distinctive "look" you'll want to employ on all job-related correspondence. A simple way to do this is to use the built-in templates that come with your word processing program. But it also might be fun to develop your own—as long as you don't get too creative! Keep type faces and design elements to a minimum. One of the best ways to achieve a balanced look and design is to choose one single display font that can be used to highlight your name or other headline-oriented material. Helvetica Bold is one good display font. Then you want to select a second font, a serif font, that is highly readable. A serif face font (such as Times Roman) is easy on the eyes, because the embellishments on the letters are proven to "lead" your eye to the next letter.

The type size of the body of your cover letter might employ an 11 point serif type with limited bolding. Nowadays, you should stay away from underlining and italics on both resumes and cover letters—these features can make your documents difficult to scan into resume databases, a significant disadvantage in the electronic age! (The same cautionary note applies to those who are tempted to submit resumes and cover letters that employ many different fonts; in addition to being difficult for humans to read, these documents also have a tendency to leave computers bewildered!)

Whether you set up your own letter style or use those that come with your word-processing program, remember to keep your style consistent whenever you use faxes, letters of confirmation, and thank-you notes. These should all be consistent in their style as well as the type of paper selected.

Don't forget to leave plenty of "white space" on your resumes and cover letters. You want your written materials to be instantly accessible, not cramped and overcrowded. (Who wants to read a page crammed with tiny type?) Keep your type spaced nicely on the page. Make it easy for the person perusing your documents to move from point to point.

And finally, remember that the most economical employment documents are usually those prospective employers read first. Don't feel you have to share *everything*—only the material likely to elicit interest in an honest, compelling way. You've got lots of information to dish out—save some of it for the interview itself!

# Cover letter don'ts

We've already briefly discussed the biggest no-no of all: excluding a cover letter entirely when mailing out a resume. Sending a cover letter is more than common courtesy—the letter adds context and a human touch for the sake of the person reviewing a resume. It's your chance to say, "This is me, on paper, outside of the formal world of my resume." Job-seekers make several other common mistakes on the cover-letter front:

- They explain every conceivable reason why the person who's reading the letter should grant them an interview. (Life is short, and so is your reader's patience. Keep it brief.)

- They believe that they must phrase the cover letter in exactly the "right" way—which is apparently a vaguely official-sounding hybrid of bureaucrat-speak. They bog down their cover letters with overused phrases such as: "Attached please find my resume..." or "Submitted for your consideration; I am responding to the advertisement in the January 18th Podunk *Globe...*" or "Enclosed you will find my resume...." There is no benefit in looking and sounding exactly like everyone else in the pile.

- They overuse the personal pronoun "I" in sentences that don't highlight solutions for the reader. (Sad but true: The reader is less concerned with you than with the problems he or she faces.)

# Doing a cover letter *right*

Target the cover letter to the research you've uncovered about the organization, and use it as a written introduction for your resume. To the degree that you can, you must make sure your cover letter is *customized.* The letter should also make brief reference to past events or conversations you've had with your contact, or to third parties who have referred you to your contact.

Two or three short, accessible, and relevant paragraphs will pack more punch for a busy reader than six densely worded paragraphs. (Many hiring managers refer to those longer letters as "life story" cover letters—and skip over them without even reading a word.) Take advantage of the work you've done to identify success stories, the benefits of hiring you, or your outstanding skills. Keep the letter short, to the point, and direct.

Without knowing much about the reader's background or personal style, you're going to have to assume a tone that's professional without being didactic or boring. Imagine that the person is zipping through a huge stack of resumes with cover letters that all read "Enclosed please find my resume," "Enclosed please find my resume," "Enclosed please find my resume"—and suddenly reads a letter that opens: "I was able to turn around a slumping sales department in just 90 days. I took our revenues from 26th to first in the division. Looking at Shore Company's product line, I feel I can do the same for you."

Okay, so you noticed in this example, the first sentence begins with the word "I." Didn't I tell you earlier to *avoid* the use if "I"? You caught me—*but...*"I" can be a powerful word, if you use it correctly! In this case, you are talking about what you have been able to accomplish, and the possibilities your candidacy brings with it. Contrast this to the more self-absorbed use of the "I" in the following sentence: "I would like to take this opportunity to introduce myself to your company." What viable information is conveyed in that statement? What phrase within it is going to motivate the reader to move your resume into the smaller pile?

You want the reviewer to be engaged with your cover letter, to ask questions, to get curious about results you'd be able to deliver for him or her. You want to interrupt the treadmill of routine and jolt the reader a little with a tantalizing reference to one of your success stories—or perhaps a bulleted list concisely summarizing two or three relevant accomplishments. The objective is to get the person to stop and ask, "How can I get this person to get these great results for *me*?"

A third-party endorsement can also bring your letter and resume to the top of the pile: "Seventeen of the top 25 Widget Assembly programs cited by *Engineering Monthly* as the best of the year were designs that I had worked at while I was at ABC Company." Here you have the advantage of an objective, recognized authority publicly acknowledging respect for your work! If you've got such a reference in your files, you should consider making use of it in your cover letter.

Perhaps even a quote from a former boss or current co-worker on your habit of working miracles would be in order. Just be sure to quote people accurately—and be sure they know they're being quoted!

A great way to get a third-party endorsement is to call and ask someone who has issued a casual compliment to put it into writing for you—or give you permission to commit the compliment to writing. You might call the person and say: "Remember when we were talking and you said that I was a superior salesman? Would you mind if I used that in some of my job search materials?"

Another effective way to gain the reviewer's attention is referring to a mutual contact. "Ed Jones over at ABC Corporation suggested that I speak with you about your opening for a Widget Polisher." This person may carry some weight with, or be a personal friend of, the interviewer; he may be someone whose opinions are well-respected in the industry. Such a reference gives your cover letter added weight, and is another way to help it to stand out from the pack.

Another compelling opening statement might be made along the following lines: "Over the past 90 days, I've been studying your company's competitive position, and I've developed a series of recommendations that I think are going to be helpful for you as you try to expand into the southeastern region. I understand from your annual report that this is one of the key goals for the upcoming quarter."

What benefit can you bring to the prospective employer's day? Did you write an article or teach a class on an area of interest to the interviewer? Do you have a solution that has worked in a situation similar to one your target company faces? Pointing out these achievements may earn you respect as an authority in your field. (News flash: If you've got expertise in solving a particular problem, you're an expert in that field!) Give the reviewer an incentive to call you. Take the initiative to study the company and offer something of measurable value, something that your competitors, in all likelihood, are not offering.

If you fail to give the reviewer a compelling reason to read your cover letter, your resume may never be read at all! You will run the risk of coming off as a carbon copy of the "average applicant"—more or less identical to all the other resumes on the desk.

Even if the reader does manage to make it through to the text of your resume in such a situation, it will almost certainly not get the attention it deserves. Without an effective cover letter to set the stage and pique curiosity, all the work you put into your resume may be for naught.

Michelle Avery of WSA Corp, one of the nation's leading career specialists, rightly points out that your cover letter must address two possible constituencies: your intended reader, and the administrative or support person helping him or her manage resume traffic. "For advertised or unadvertised openings," Michelle advises, "you have to keep it short. The people who handle your letter and resume are usually bombarded with resumes, and if you don't get their attention right away, you're likely to be passed over. In cover letters for our clients, we try to focus on one compelling accomplishment—a revenue increase, a cost decrease, or a savings in time—that the person reading the letter can scan more or less instantly.

"Brevity is particularly important if you're writing to someone who's got a secretary or assistant opening the mail. The aim there is to pose a question or raise an issue that the administrative person can't resolve independently, and to do it in just a few sentences. That increases the likelihood of your cover letter and resume making it through to your intended reader."

Avery suggests avoiding long-winded explanations of *why* you are currently engaged in a job search, *how* you're approaching that search, or *where* you heard about the opening—and instead spotlighting "bottom-line" issues of direct interest to the hiring manager. One such appeal might sound like this: "Do you know of anyone who'd be interested in speaking with a salesperson who's exceeded quota every year for the past six years?"

Pose short questions or develop concise statements that practically *force* the hiring manager to turn the page and take a look at your resume. Get right to the point in your cover letter; assume that this person stayed at work late to review the resumes that couldn't be squeezed into the regular day's work. (Often, this is the case!) Assume that your reader is eager to get home—and is merely skimming your letter. He or she is looking for one or two good matches before heading home; make sure your letter makes that connection!

# Do I call you or do you call me?

What's the next step you want your reader to follow after he or she reads your cover letter? How do you plan to connect with the prospective employer? And what should you say about this at the end of your letter?

The passive approach is simply to say that you will look forward to a call. There's nothing wrong with that, as long as you don't waste too much time and energy staring at the phone and trying to make it ring. You can always place a follow-up call if you haven't heard from your contact within a day or so.

A more assertive approach is to mention your plan to call the contact on a specific date. (This was the approach you saw in the Talent Match letter.) In this way, you relieve the interviewer of the responsibility of tracking you down, and you initiate action. Your own preferences, and the degree to which tactful personal assertiveness may be required in the job you're trying to win, should dictate the strategy you select. (Some sales managers have been known to test the tenacity and follow-through of aspiring sales candidates by testing which applicant is most energetic in initiating phone calls to discuss current openings.)

If you opt to take the initiative to follow up on your own, one effective strategy is to state when you'll be calling at the end of the cover letter, in a P.S. statement. Chances are that the P.S., unusual in a cover letter, will grab the interviewer's attention immediately. So you might add to your letter: "I'll plan on calling you Thursday morning between 9 and 10. In the meantime, if you have any questions or want to get in touch with me sooner, please don't hesitate to call me at..."

As with your Talent Match letter, the only rule to follow on this score is *always* to call when you say you'll call! To fail to follow up on such a promise will jeopardize your credibility.

# Getting creative

Your goal in developing your cover letter is to write something that resonates perfectly with what's already on your reader's mind. This may be relatively easy to do—if you have some direct knowledge of the interviewer. Perhaps you have a contact who has tipped you off to the fact that the interviewer is a rabid Boston Red Sox fan, or perhaps this fact came up during your phone conversations. You might consider working in a one-liner that briefly mentions the team's recent fortunes, and then make reference to your own stellar team spirit and a recent "home run" you hit on the job!

You shouldn't be afraid to try something new or unconventional in your cover letter—but you should stay away from "tricks" likely to be perceived as tasteless. A little bit of imagination and ingenuity can display welcome evidence of personality (a trait often in short supply in employment correspondence) make the reader curious, and go a long way in getting your hired.

Here you may want to refer to my book *303 Off The Wall Ways to Get a Job.* In researching this book I found several people who used highly creative approaches in their cover letters. These inventive cover letters could stand alone, without a resume. Consider the following, from Massachusetts writer Michelle Simos, reprinted from my book:

> It's three a.m. in the big city. We've been watching apartment #245 near the alley at Twenty-fifty and Sixth since 10:25 this morning. We're four-and-a-half hours into the stakeout and have nothing to report. "What's that?" I ask as I withdraw my loaded gun from my holster and shake my partner. (His name's Tuesday. I'm

Friday. Today's Wednesday.) But on closer inspection, we realize it's only two pigeons picking through the contents of a steel-gray dumpster. "This surveillance stuff is really for the birds," I think to myself. Then the screen door opens—and she slips discreetly out the front door and quickly rounds the corner. We're right behind her when, mysteriously, she vanishes before our very eyes.

Don't make the same mistake as Sgt. Friday. Your chance to snag an ace managing editor is within reach. This seasoned, creative writer, meticulous editor and re-sults-oriented project manager would like to meet with you to discuss your paper's new magazine venture.

(Reprinted from *303 Off-the-Wall Ways to Get a Job*, Brandon Toropov, Career Press, 1996.)

A targeted approach like this, delivered to the right company, can help make you stand out from the crowd and leave a powerful first impression. Unfortunately, you can't always use such a letter—some large and/or conservative firms (such as a major energy company, or an old and prestigious law firm) are unlikely to respond well to crea-tive employment appeals. But at smaller, entrepreneurial businesses, where such creativity is likely to be appreciated as a major asset, this approach may be worth a try.

Whether you are preparing a highly creative cover letter or you are following a more traditional writing approach, remember that your goal is to stand out from the competition! *Do not* litter your cover letter with stock phrases and references to *your* goals. In your cover letter—not to mention any other communication piece that's part of your job-search strategy—you want to solve the problems and fulfill the needs of your reader, the employer, and the company. As you craft your cover letter, and develop your mailing package, keep the unique needs and interests of your prospective employer at the forefront of your thoughts.

# CHAPTER 7

# Mailing Your Package for Maximum Effect

*"Those who work with their minds govern those who work with their bodies."*

—Mencius, Chinese philosopher

Now that you've gotten a good idea of the requirements of the job you're pursuing, compiled relevant success stores, established the look of your key documents, and developed an interview-winning cover letter, it's time to focus on the various contact strategies that will help you win an in-person interview in a hurry. In this chapter, you'll learn how to sequence your mailing for maximum effect.

Again: You are trying to get on the hiring manager's radar screen, and the best way to do that is usually to (Plan A) pick up the phone and ask for the chance to get together. If you are unable to get a face-to-face meeting, you will want to (Plan B) try to obtain, over the phone, the hiring manager's personal goals in filling the position, or at least some of the job's key requirements. Both of these appeals are designed to help you develop information that will allow you to set up a customized resume, which you can then either mail or offer to deliver in person.

If both of these efforts fail, you will want to (Plan C) mail your Talent Match letter—making sure to include a brief reference to your phone conversation—to your contact, and then follow up by phone as promised at the conclusion of that letter. Throughout the process, you will be on the lookout for specific information that will help you to target your resume. Your Talent Match letter, under some circumstances, can become a "talking paper" that can be used to obtain additional information for the customized resume you will need to develop for later discussions.

# Then what?

So—you mail your Talent Match letter, and the day and time you specified for your follow-up call rolls around. Your order of priorities at that point is:

*1. Ask for an in-person meeting.* Call the person on the date and time specified in your Talent Match letter and ask for 30 to 45 minutes of his or her time to discuss the position you are seeking. It is a good idea to take the initiative in setting up the interview. Suggest a specific day and time.

Beware! If you find yourself being asked about your job history, the challenges you've met, and the salary you're looking for—you have entered into a phone interview! This is a convenience for the interviewer, but it must be managed deftly. An in-depth phone interview, where the goal is usually to knock candidates out of the running, is seldom in your best interests. A face-to-face interview offers you far more opportunity to display your strong suits.

The best strategy for handling a phone interview is to give a concise, accurate answer to the question at hand—and then return to your request for an in-person meeting. It might sound like this:

**Contact**:

"Tell me—how do you feel about working under deadlines?"

**You:**

"Well, we had some very tight schedules at ABC Company, but I always found those to be a challenge, and I think that the challenge of working under a tight deadline is one of the things that I do best." (This answer doesn't give the interviewer many variables to pull apart.)

"You know, Mr. Gonzalez, I've done a lot of research on this opportunity and I think it makes a lot of sense for you and me to get together and talk about this in more detail. Can we get together Monday morning at a convenient time for you?"

Again, remain goal-oriented and conclude your response by making a very specific request.

There is simply no advantage for you in going along with an in-depth phone interview, and every advantage in trying, politely and tactfully, to gain a face-to-face meeting. Most people who are interviewed over the phone are knocked out of the process, saving the interviewer time—but short-changing the applicant.

You may wish to request a meeting to discuss subjects *other* than the job opening—such as the competitive challenges the company currently faces, or the possibility of freelance work. (Some applicants have found that offering to take the hiring official to lunch at a nearby restaurant is a good way to schedule these kinds of discussions.)

**2. If you fail to obtain a commitment for a meeting, ask if it's possible for you to simply swing by and drop off your resume in person.** A decision-maker who meets face-to-face with you, looks you in the eye, and takes this sheet of paper from you—even a resume that is not as targeted as it could be—is far more likely to want to learn more about you. If nothing else happens when you drop the resume off than actually meeting the potential interviewer, you will have accomplished a fair amount!

You might phrase your request as follows:

"Mr. Jones, I understand how busy you are right now, but I'm going to be in your neighborhood next week. What I'd like to know is if it would be possible for me to swing by and drop off my resume sometime over the next couple of days. Would 2:30 on Tuesday be okay with you? It would only take us a minute or two, and I'd really love to see your operation in person."

It is important to be specific about the date and time. Bear in mind that a professional, polished, and persistent approach works best. After all, you are (potentially) beginning a relationship with a new boss!

**3. If you strike out there, lay the groundwork for mailing your resume and cover letter without an in-person meeting.** If you must mail your resume rather than deliver it in person, don't mail materials that will look like everyone else's! In the event that you aren't able to obtain an in-person interview, ask the hiring person to give you a little more information about the problems he or she faces—the problems that have given rise to the opening. Then use this information in your targeted resume and cover letter (based on one of the samples that appear in the second half of this book). Customize your approach as much as possible; try to use text that will remind your reader that you and he spoke. ("Thank you again for taking time out of your busy day to talk about the opening for a publishing assistant; I hope your meetings with the national sales staff went well.")

***4. No matter what happens, stay upbeat.*** The goal through-out this process is to stay active, to help move the process forward. You will probably want to prepare some questions ahead of time to ask your potential interviewer. No matter which category your call falls into, you may want to prepare questions that get your contact's views on issues you've already researched in one form or another:

- What do you feel the most important duties of this position are?

- What has been the biggest challenge in this area in the past?

- I understand from the company's mission statement that the goal is to expand the engineering department over the next five years. In what areas is this likely to be done?

- What effect do you think the present economic (slump/growth) in East Wherever will have on the company's international sales?

- What new products is the company looking to develop with respect to X competitor?

- What's the main thing you want your new employee to accomplish for you?

Your goal is to develop a few key questions that will give you insights into the position and help you develop a sound interviewing strategy for later. If it's at all possible to do so, you should try to de-velop your resume based on the feedback you receive from your en-counter with a prospective employer.

At any point during the calling process, you can expect your contact to launch a "prove-it-to-me" question. ("Tell me a little bit about yourself" is a common "prove-it-to-me" question.) This query is a request that you demonstrate that the time spent with you during an in-person meeting will be worthwhile for both parties. In other words, you have one shot, one opportunity to make your case for an in-person meeting. You could begin your response by saying something like this:

> "I'm currently working in the Widget Polishing Division at ABC Corporation, and I understand there's an opening at your firm for a Widget Engineer. While working as a widget polisher, I studied engineering at night school. I graduated with a 3.7 average and contributed to the successful launch of the Widget Polishing Quarterly Review System at ABC. I was able to help lower operating costs in widget polishing by 9 percent by utilizing the engineering department at an earlier stage of production. I appreciate your taking the time to talk to me about this opportunity; and I would really like to get your feedback about the job, because I believe I have a lot to offer. Could we get together on Monday?"

You have just combined three concise summaries of the success stories you've developed—and you've demonstrated that you meet the requirements of the position, as far as you've been able to determine them. You have been successful in the areas of change, profit, and sales, and you're asking for a chance to talk in greater depth about the opening.

# What's not to like?

The goal is to get noticed—and the best way to get there is through a professional, persistent, and polite approach. One great way to do this is to keep the details of one compelling story coming until you get a response one way or the other.

Some people won't respond positively the first time around. That's okay. With regular mail, your fax, e-mail, and the phone, you can adapt "teaser" messages from your cover letter, built around a condensed version of the success story that most clearly exemplifies your best qualifications for the particular job. Pass along a message that examines one of your success stories in-depth. If you're leaving a voice-mail message, you could decide to leave one like this:

> "Hi. This is Jane Daniels. On my last job, I found $225,000 worth of excess expenses due to overlapping accounting systems. I was able to eliminate those, manage the inventory a little bit better, and save that much money for my company. I think we should explore the possibility that I could deliver the same types of results for your firm. My number is.... Please give me a call."

That's a concise summary of a success story that you may want to put out on all fronts. Adapt your cover letter. (Remember: There are plenty of models in the second half of the book that will help you develop a new winning cover letter in next to no time.) Leave your contact a fax message with your phone number; connect by phone; leave a creative voice-mail message...and, if you can track down the appropriate e-mail address, send your story there, too!

Whatever strategy you choose to follow in launching your job-search campaign, remember that there's nothing to apologize for in taking the initiative to follow up appropriately. Once you have established the right mailing and calling sequence, pursue it with confidence and optimism.

# CHAPTER 8

# Some Thoughts on Rejection: Turning Lemons into Lemonade

*"Let me tell you the secret that has led me to my goal. My strength lies solely in my tenacity."*
—Louis Pasteur, 19th-century French scientist

$M$ost people believe that a rejection letter is final, the end of the road. You may believe that an interviewer's past "no" represents that organization's final judgment on your abilities. You won an interview and were under serious consideration, but you got "shot down." Or did you?

If you had an in-person interview, that's an excellent sign. The interviewer was impressed enough with your qualifications, your cover letter, your resume, and your presentation to make an appointment to meet with you in person. He or she may have considered you to be a likely candidate given the solutions you provided for past employers and the other success stories you presented from your background. It is usually the case that there are several qualified applicants for one position. Unfortunately, talented people are often turned away.

You were fortunate enough to have had an interview; you liked what you saw, and felt that you received some positive feedback from the interviewer. This means that you now have, not simply a rejection letter, but also an established contact within an organization. Unlike 90 percent of the people who applied for the position, you got an interview. It's often difficult to get an interview. For most of us, there are a lot more "no's" than "yes's" on the way to a face-to-face meeting.

It's very rare for an interviewer to decide he or she simply never wants to see you again. I know. I used to be a manager in charge of interviewing applicants. On several occasions, I had people whom I had previously turned down come back to me over the next few weeks or months and say, "I spoke with you a while back about the opening for such-and-such a job, and I just wanted to see if there is anything else that might be open now." This is a powerful and persuasive appeal demonstrating tenacity and a strong interest in the company.

You're playing a numbers game. You need one job. The right company, once you find it, needs one employee. Although the interviewer may be interested in your qualifications, the organization he or she works for may have only one slot that's right for you *at the present time*. Five days from now, the situation may be completely different. Today, valuable contacts can be made on the employment front almost instantly, but they can be lost just as quickly if you don't attend to them!

The "no" that is staring you in the face today may be the lead that will get you a "yes" tomorrow. You have made a contact, and the person you dealt with knows who you are. A positive assessment of the situation says, "I'm now on this person's radar screen. Even though I've gotten a 'no' for now, even though I've gotten a letter back that says, 'Sorry, but we selected another candidate,' I have at least made a contact." Here is someone who has taken valuable time out of a busy workday to speak with you, arrange an interview, and talk over the pros and cons of what you have to offer.

So, stay in touch! Take all of your "no" answers and create a new file: "*Rejection Letters/Contacts*" for use later in your job search. This file of existing "no's" holds a potential gold mine. Perhaps you can turn one of these "no's" into a "yes." Why not call back and find out where things stand after a week or two has passed?

There may have been changes or growth in the organization where a new place for your talents has been created or vacated. Perhaps you have learned a new way to sell your skills, perhaps changes in the industry have created a new job category, or maybe you can offer to take a course and get more training while the employer works with you on a project basis. When in doubt, ask!

Not every "no" can be turned into a "yes," but it's almost unheard of to reach a "yes" without hearing a few "no's" during a job search. You are now in the world of marketing, and your chief product is yourself. The process of selling anything involves rejections. It's about knocking on doors, and being willing to check back with prospects who said "no" a while back to find out what the situation looks like now. If you make enough of these calls, you will dramatically increase the likelihood of converting a "no" into a "yes."

I'm not suggesting that focusing *exclusively* on rejections is the way to go, but I am suggesting that, while you continue to search for new opportunities, you shouldn't neglect the work you've already done. Go through your rejections and consider the goodwill that you have developed from your face-to-face meetings. Call the contact with whom you felt most comfortable. Ask what's up; find out what new things this person is trying to get accomplished. Consider inviting the person to lunch for an informal discussion about opportunities in the industry. If your contact does not have an opening to discuss, perhaps he or she knows of someone who does. Following up politely and persistently will usually convince your contact of your initiative and professionalism, and encourage him or her to take action on your behalf.

# CHAPTER 9

# 10 Final Words to the Wise

*"Individuality is consciousness of will, to be conscious that you have a will and can act."*

—Katherine Mansfield, 20th-century British writer

You're almost there! You've learned about identifying goals, conducting a last-minute research campaign, creating a Talent Match letter, developing an effective cover letter, establishing the perfect look for your correspondence, setting up a schedule that makes sense for your mailing, and even dealing with rejection. But watch out! Especially when time is tight, it's easy to make a tactical error as you embark on your last-minute job search. Read this chapter carefully—and review it as often as necessary—to avoid these common obstacles to cover letter success. With apologies to the home office at the Ed Sullivan Theater in New York:

# Top 10 Things
## *Not* to Do When You Need to Put Together a Top-Notch Cover Letter in a Hurry

**#10.** Create a single impersonal "all-purpose" letter, then photocopy it for use in every job lead you pursue.

**#9.** Jam the cover letter with so much text that the reader needs a magnifying glass to make it out

**#8.** Compose a cover letter that requires more than one page.

**#7.** Fail to target your resume package with a cover letter customized for the receiver. Both your cover letter and your resume, as well as any supporting documentation you choose to send along, should be targeted to the needs of a particular employer.

**#6.** Get chummy, or use inappropriate language. "Hey pardner! I've got a hell of a proposition for you! Put me to work!"

**#5.** Use so many fonts that the reader thinks he's just received a ransom note.

**#4.** Send in a document that fairly screams "amateur." Cover letters have reached employers written on lined notebook paper, marred with dozens of hand-scrawled corrections, or doused with perfume. None of this makes a positive impression.

**#3.** Misspell the contact's name. Sure, it's easy to do when you have a lot of leads to pursue—but it costs you big time. Many managers will simply ignore anything and everything that follows if their name is misspelled in the cover letter. Call ahead and get the right spelling and pronunciation!

**#2.** Send the letter off without having someone else proof it. Even a computerized spell-checker can miss typos that may make you look like a bonehead.

**#1.** Send the resume and letter off without attempting to make some kind of personal contact with your reader first.

# PART II

## SAMPLE COVER LETTERS

Here they are—powerful, dramatic, concise cover letters written for applicants in a wide variety of fields. Pick one or several that seem to match your needs. You can adapt these versions quickly and easily to your own last-minute job search.

Many of the letters that follow were developed by some of the country's top employment specialists to speed up the job-search campaigns of their clients. You can use the fruits of these labors now—and develop a superior written employment appeal that's fully customized to your situation in next to no time.

After this section, you will find an appendix that offers models for two vitally important pieces of correspondence—the Talent Match letter (discussed in the first half of this book) and the post-interview thank-you letter. In addition, you'll find information on how to get in touch with resume and cover letter writers who are among the most distinguished in their fields of specialty.

Alan McGill
0 Bay Club Drive, Apt. 00
Bayside, New York 11360
(718) 000-0000

January 26, 1999

Jane Martin
Smithside Hospital
410 Lakeville Road
Smith Park, NY 11040

Dear Ms. Martin:

As someone who successfully operated a manufacturing business in the frenetically paced garment center prior to completing work on my degree, I possess an excellent blend of practical working experience along with a distinguished academic background. Having recently completed the requirements for a B.A. in Accounting and Information Systems at Carter College, my aim is to make an immediate contribution as an entry-level accountant at Smithside Hospital.

Enclosed is a copy of my resume. I look forward to meeting with you to discuss my qualifications for an accounting position with Smithside.

Sincerely,


Alan McGill

Enclosure

Betty Ames
000-00 Maple Avenue
Flushing, New York 11355
(718) 000-0000

January 26, 1999

To:    Ellen Jones
Re:    Administrative Assistant Opening

Dear Ms. Jones:

Terry Martin suggested I pass along the enclosed resume in reference to the above opening.

I am a detail-oriented professional with extensive experience in all major IBM and Apple office software applications, eleven years of experience in coordinating the schedules and correspondence of mid- and top-level executives, and references that describe me as "the best thing that ever happened to our office" and "a walking productivity seminar."

I will call you next week; perhaps we can set up an appointment to discuss this opportunity.

Sincerely,


Betty Ames

Enc.: Resume

**MICHAEL A. WILLIAMS**
00-00 Horace Harding Expressway
Ardsley Avenue, New York 11368
(718) 000-0000

September 11, 1998

Mr. James Dorsal
Mammal Department
High Side Zoo
Southern Boulevard
Bronx, NY 10460

Dear Mr. Dorsal:

Thanks for taking the time to speak with me this afternoon.

You asked for a copy of my resume, which is enclosed, and some more background about my academic work. I graduated from John Bowne High School in June, 1994 with an agriculture certified diploma and a perfect attendance record over four years. I am presently enrolled in Brooklyn College pursuing a biology degree, with a minor in computer science. I will graduate in May of this year.

As noted in my resume, my experience has focused on the study and care of animals. I feel that this knowledge and experience will benefit the mammal department, as will my strong commitment to the critical goals of conservation and rehabilitation of wildlife. (I am a weekly volunteer with AmeriClean; project director Judy McKinney describes my work as "superior in every way.")

I would welcome the opportunity to meet with you personally to discuss employment opportunities.

Sincerely yours,


Michael A. Williams

enc.

Mark Evers
2209 Cambridge Street
Cambridge, MA 13098
(617) 555-5555


May 23, 1999


Ms. Francine Daniels
Lewiston International
22 Boylston Street
Boston, MA 02107

Dear Ms. Daniels:

As an art dealer for McKay and Company, I helped to set a new record for annual revenue in our Boston location. My research indicates that your firm is eager to grow, and that my experience in developing relationships with high-net-worth collectors could be an asset to your firm.

I'm enclosing my resume; if you are interested in meeting with someone with a record of superior achievement in selling fine works of art, we should meet. I will call you Friday morning to introduce myself and talk further. In the meantime, please don't hesitate to call me if you have any questions about my experiences.

Sincerely,


Mark Evers

Enc.

Debbie James
453 Tip Boulevard
Rowley, MA 11102
(555) 000-0000


October 17, 1998


Mr. Terence Rose
Human Resources Department
Deer Health Care Center
1055 5th Avenue
Brooklyn, NY 10029

Dear Mr. Rose:

The billing position we discussed seems like a perfect match with my skills. I have completed an extensive Certified Medical Assistant program at the Yardley School of Allied Health; I have experience in medical billing, phlebotomy, and EKG procedures (my current manager calls the "the wizard" in reference to these areas) and I am computer literate.

As you requested, I have enclosed my resume, which will give you a detailed background of my qualifications. I would like to schedule an appointment to meet you to discuss this matter. I can be reached at (555) 000-0000, Monday through Friday 9 a.m. to 5 p.m. I look forward to having an interview with you.

Sincerely,


Debbie James

Enclosure

Mary Jones
00-00 000th Street
Queens Village, NY 11429
(718) 000-0000


February 28, 1999


Lauren McRiley, Administrator
All Together Health Care Services
987 Square One Plaza
Highside, NY 11801

Dear Ms. McRiley:

Thank you for taking the time to speak to me about the position of Branch Manager at the Highside Office. I learned a great deal and know that I would be able to make an immediate positive contribution to your prestigious organization.

As I mentioned, I currently work as office manager for Nelson Associates. By changing temporary staffing services, I was able to reduce our expenditures in this area by 19 percent—while increasing overall productivity.

Enclosed is a copy of my resume to provide you more detail about my experiences. If you have any further questions, don't hesitate to contact me.

Sincerely,


Mary Jones

Enclosure

**CAROL LONGLEY**
**116 Fox Road**
**Springfield, PA 19064**
**610-322-1456**

January 7, 1999

Mr. Trumore
Brooks Company
6557 Filmore Road
Springfield, PA 19065

Dear Mr. Trumore:

Twelve years of experience in marketing and major brand management for a Fortune 100 company is the background I can bring to your organization.

Consider the following credentials:

- Major Brands Manager: Achieved record sales/earnings for major product line.
- Product Manager: Repositioned failing line and increased sales by 235% in a two-year period.
- Marketing Manager: Exceeded sales targets each year by an average of 28%.
- M.B.A., Marketing, Riverside School of Business
- B.S., Business Administration, Brooksby University

If you have a need for an innovative manager with my experience, please call me.

Sincerely yours,

Carol Longley

Enc.

DAVID TRISNER
1239 West End Avenue
New York, NY 11290
(212) 555-5786

August 14, 1998

Mr. Brian Miller
Miller's Restaurant
198 Broadway
New York, NY 11297

Dear Mr. Miller:

Let me know if you're interested in working with a chef whose menu selection and food preparation techniques were praised in *The New York Times* as "innovative and completely satisfying." (March 23, 1998).

I've done quite a bit of research on your chain in recent days, and would be eager to discuss your expansion into the Boston area. If the enclosed resume is of interest to you, please call me.

Sincerely,


David Trisner

Enclosure

Samuel Clarke
00 Clarke Street
Long Beach, NY 11561
(718) 000-0000


July 14, 1998

Janis Smith
ABC Corporation
123 Main Street
Long Beach, NY 11501

Dear Ms. Smith:

Would your search for a Chief of Security benefit from a discussion with a seasoned executive with more than 11 years of experience, three industry awards, and a commitment to discovering cutting-edge solutions to operational and security problems?

My resume (enclosed) explains that I have had experience in maintaining corporate security and was responsible for the development of emergency evacuation procedures at a major chemical processing operation. In addition, I have had the opportunity to develop skills so important to the smooth and successful coordination of operations. These skills are highly transferable to many situations.

I look forward to speaking with you.

Sincerely,


Samuel Clarke

Enclosure

Ellen Morrison
343 Huntington Avenue
Boston, MA 02127
(617) 555-5555

December 8, 1998

Martin Schuster
Schuster Industries
146 Boylston Street
Boston, MA 02127

Dear Mr. Schuster:

Jane Martin, in your Cambridge office, told me that you were always interested in talking to good civil engineers.

I've been responsible for design and documentation on a wide variety of challenging and rewarding projects. Recently, I completed a design on the stormwater drainage design element of the recent Conrad Towers project, praised by an industry magazine as "some of the most innovative design work we've seen in some time." I like to think that the clarity and care of my design was one reason the project came in on time and under budget.

If the enclosed resume is of interest to you, perhaps we should meet in person. I will call you Monday morning, December 14, to introduce myself and see whether we can arrange a meeting.

Sincerely,

Ellen Morrison

Enclosure

Jane Doerman
106 Winter Street, Apt. 25H
Evanston, IL 11300
(516) 555-5555

August 10, 1998

Alexander P. Morrison
Vice President of Marketing and Clinical Affairs
Mira Medical, Inc.
109 60th Street, Suite 408
Chicago, IL 11788

Dear Mr. Morrison:

Sincerest thanks for taking so much time from your busy schedule to talk with me today to discuss the opportunities at Mira Medical as Clinical Manager.

In my experience, clinical support has proven invaluable in promoting product credibility and user loyalty. This clinical support must, of course, be part of a team effort. I feel very strongly that I can be a valuable member of the Mira Medical team as it moves into the future. In my current position, I have developed similar programs that have helped to launch brands now representing more than $10 million in annual revenue.

Thank you again for your time and consideration, and I look forward to our next conversation.

Sincerely yours,

Jane Doerman

Enclosure

Michael Risby
3008 Main Drive
Brooklyn, NY 11204
(718) 555-5555


November 16, 1998


Jonathan Enders
FTP International, Limited
346 Atlantic Avenue
Brooklyn, NY 11203

Dear Mr. Enders:

Let me know if you would like to discuss the way I implemented a new accounts receivables program for my current employer—a program that resulted in an average payment improvement of 17 days, and helped to reduce bad debt by 19%.

If the enclosed resume is not of interest to you, would you please pass it along to someone who would benefit from my experience in streamlining financial systems for maximum profitability?

Sincerely,


Michael Risby

Enclosure

Marilyn Jones
55-55 Elm Avenue
Forner, NY 11358
(718) 000-0000


March 10, 1999


Ms. Carolyn Jones, Director, Counseling Center
Johnson Institute of Technology
1026 Riverside Drive
New York, NY 10001

Dear Ms. Jones:

Thanks for discussing your opening for a counselor with me today.  My familiarity with and dedication to the J.I.T. community as an employee for 13 years gives me some unique insights on this position.

The positive feedback from my counseling experience at N.Y.U., along with my independent work counseling students in the placement office at J.I.T., would benefit your department dramatically.

Thank you for your consideration.  I look forward to speaking with  you.

Sincerely yours,



Marilyn Jones

Enclosures

**GRACE PETERSON**
40–42 45th Street
Jackson Heights, New York 11370
(718) 000-0000

August 8, 1998

Melanie Swanson
Human Resources
New York Journal
229 West 43rd Street
New York, NY 10036

Dear Ms. Swanson:

As credit manager for Rightway Corporation, I was able to reduce our quarterly bad debt rate by 35%. I'd like to meet with you personally to explain how I did it.

I feel certain you will welcome the contributions I can make to the *Journal*. You can reach me during business hours at (516) 000-0000 ext. 226.

Thank you for your interest.

Sincerely,


Grace Peterson

Enclosure

Danielle Johnson
55 Buena Vista Drive, Apt #6
Santa Fe, New Mexico  01387
(405) 555-8899


September 5, 1998


Mr. Mark Evans
New Dimensions, International
33-78 Riverview Boulevard
Santa Fe, New Mexico 02744

Dear Mr. Evans:

Let me know if your organization would benefit from working with an experienced customer service supervisor who reduced requests for refunds on a key new product release by 17% in just three months.

The details are featured in my resume (enclosed)—please contact me if you are interested in discussing New Dimensions' plans for launching the customer service center here in Santa Fe.

Sincerely,


Danielle Johnson

Enc.

John W. Jones
00-000 Forest Avenue
Miami, Florida 55555
(999) 555-9999

July 19, 1998

Ms. Jennifer Page
ABC Air
P.O. Box 555
Miami, FL 55555

Dear Ms. Page:

Thank you for forwarding the candidate information pack in connection with the new position of Manager of Customer Service at ABC Air. As you requested, I'm enclosing my resume.

Manager of Customer Service was one of the positions I held at Fly Away Fast Airways during the 17 years I was employed there. I was named "Supervisor of the Year" three times while at Fly Away Fast for launching innovative customer retention programs.

I look forward to speaking with you about this opportunity. I will call you Friday morning July 24, to see if we can arrange a meeting.

Sincerely,

John W. Jones

Enclosure

John C. Jones
P.O. Box 1056
West Roxbury, MA 02111
(617) 555-0000


July 10, 1998

Ms. Tina True
Human Resources Specialist
Massachusetts Transit Authority
204 Ridge Street, Room 409
Boston, MA 02111

Posting Number: 97-348 (TA)

Dear Ms. True:

 Are you interested in speaking with someone who can put 21 years of rapid transit operational experience to work as a Deputy Superintendent?

 My employment with the Transit Authority has been marked by consistently increasing levels of responsibility and achievement. I am thoroughly familiar with the daily operations of the Rapid Transit System.

 If the enclosed resume is of interest to you, perhaps we could get together. I look forward to talking to you and learning more about the challenges and opportunities at Massachusetts Transit Authority.

Sincerely yours,

John D. Jones

Enclosure

**DEBBIE BROWN**
**55-55 55th Street**
**Whitestone, NY 11357**
**(718) 555-5555**

May 20, 1999

Maria Jones, Editor
Thrifty Times
100 Cheep Street
Whitestone, NY 11357

Dear Ms. Jones:

Can you use the services of a qualified desktop publishing specialist who was named "Artist of the Year" in her firm?

My three years of experience can be utilized to aid in the production of your quarterly newsletter.

Please take a moment to review my resume. If there is a suitable position available now or in the future, I'd very much appreciate the opportunity to speak with you.

Thank you for your time and consideration. I look forward to meeting with you soon.

Sincerely,


Debbie Brown

Enc. Resume

JOHN B. SMITH
18 Hatcher Lane
Cedar Brook, NJ 08018
(609) 975-5429

December 28, 1998

Ms. Sarah Drewmore
Cedar Hills, Inc.
175 Yorksville Road
Cedar Side, NJ 09183

Dear Ms. Drewmore:

Our mutual friend and colleague Stew Johnson felt my 20 years in logistics and distribution management would be of interest to you. To familiarize you a little better, let me highlight some of my accomplishments:

- Reduced inventory discrepancies by more than 37%, while increasing storage capacity by 85%.
- Featured in *Business Guide* magazine for the development of a computerized international order control and shipping system.
- Consolidated three geographically distant operations, saving 43% in overhead expense.
- Upgraded distribution output from a substandard rate to one of the highest in the entire country.

I possess exceptional strengths in work and manpower planning, quality control, warehouse design and automation, receiving, shipping, and customer service. In addition, I am acknowledged as one of the leading experts in the country at streamlining ordering and inventory tracking systems.

Recognizing that you may be difficult to reach, I will plan to contact your secretary in an effort to arrange a convenient time for us to meet. I am totally flexible and would be pleased to meet either during or outside of normal business hours.

I look forward to meeting you personally.

Sincerely,

John B. Smith

Enc.

GEORGE MESSINA
55-55 55th Street, Apt. C
Sunnyside, NY 11104
(718) 555-5555


October 13, 1998


John Smith
ABC Transport
111 Main Street
Bayridge, NY 11001

Dear Mr. Smith:

Are you looking for someone who is more concerned about what he can do for the company than what the company can do for him? Someone who is self-motivated, rather than waiting to be motivated? Someone who will work for you instead of "putting in time?"

I am skilled as a driver of 35-foot trucks. I have a spotless safety record and three "employee of the month" awards. Due to the reduction in the work force at the distribution center for Jawbreaker Ice Cream in the Major Metropolitan area, I've reentered the job market. I am thoroughly familiar with most of the major thoroughfares in the metropolitan area, Nassau and Suffolk counties, upstate New York, Connecticut, and New Jersey.

I have enclosed a resume for your perusal. I hope we can get together to discuss employment opportunities with your company.

Very truly yours,


George Messina

Enc.: Resume

Benjamin Bruce
27 East Side Drive
Denver, CO 11903
(204) 555-5555


January 13, 1999


Mark Miller
Learn-to-Drive, Inc.
1309 Drexel Drive
Denver, CO 11908

Dear Mr. Miller:

Brendan Powers, in your Denver office, mentioned that you were looking for "qualified driving instructors with excellent safety records."

I worked for Destry Driving Schools for six years, was never involved in an accident or cited for a moving violation, and helped 97% of my students pass driving tests on their first try.

Brendan led me to believe that, if the enclosed resume is not of interest to you, you will be able to pass it along to someone who would benefit from meeting someone with my background.

I look forward to hearing from you!

Sincerely,


Benjamin Bruce

Enc.

**Michael Santos**
**293 Steamboat Road**
**Greenwich, CT 12290**
**(503) 555-6688**

May 23, 1999

Ms. Stephanie Shea, President
Shea Publishing
2324 3rd Avenue
Stamford, CT 11208

Dear Ms. Shea:

Let me know if you or someone you know is interested in working with an experienced acquisitions editor who launched three of the 10 titles listed on the *Parents America* end-of-year, top-selling books for children.

My resume is enclosed; please let me know if it's of interest to you or someone you know.

Thanks!

Sincerely,

Michael Santos

Enc.

JOHN NASSER
18 Hatcher Lane
Cedar Brook, NJ 08018
(609) 555-5429

August 28, 1998

Margaret Skylar
Gopher Engineering
2098 Brooks Street
Cedar Brook, NJ 08018

Dear Ms. Skylar:

As a result of recent downsizing at my company, I feel it is time to start actively thinking about a career move. Needless to say, this decision is highly confidential, and senior management is unaware of my intention. I am seeking a managerial position in Engineering and Development with a major high-tech manufacturer.

Although I certainly would not expect you to be aware of a specific job opportunity that would fit my background, I would appreciate it if you could spend an hour or so with me over lunch. I would value any general thoughts and advice you might have concerning my job hunting campaign. I have taken the liberty of enclosing my resume for your reference.

I will call your secretary to see if I can coordinate a time that would be convenient to your schedule.

Very truly yours,

John Nasser

Enc.

John Johnson
2034 East 80th Street, Apt #4
New York, NY 11208
(212) 555-4455


January 31, 1999


Sarah Fields
Environmental Education Services
1209 West 72nd Street
New York, NY 11203

Dear Ms. Fields:

    Thanks for taking my call today. It was a pleasure discussing your opening for an Environmental Services Engineer. I understand your concern over the recent state legislating targeting the widget refurbishing industry.

    As you requested, I'm enclosing my resume. You may be particularly interested in the first item in the "Experience" section, which details my work determining cost-effective responses to develop compliance strategies for new environmental regulations that affected my current employer. Our Chief Operating Officer estimated the cost savings of our (successful) compliance campaign as approximately $1.2 million, when compared with the formal proposal submitted by an outside consultant.

Sincerely,



 John Johnson


Enc.

    P.S.: I will plan to call you on Friday morning, February 4, to discuss this opportunity.

Sarah Silverton
787 Lakewood Drive
Chicago, IL 60606
(312) 555-5762


February 2, 1999


Mario Miller
Beachside Products
2298 Washington Avenue
Chicago, IL 60606

Dear Mr. Miller:

As a designer for Rams' Horn Fashions, I launched a new line of beachwear that accounted for $2.4 million in revenues in the past fiscal year.

I've studied your company with interest in recent weeks, and would be interested in speaking with you about your company's plans to expand your swimwear line, as reported in the January issue of *Hollywood Fashion.*

If my resume (enclosed) is of interest, perhaps we could get together!

Sincerely,


Sarah Silverton

Enc.

John Ramrod
20 Sunset Lane
Cedar Brook, NJ 08018
(609) 555-5429

February 28, 1999

Mr. Robert Clark
BCA National
889 Bayside Lane
Cedar Brook, NJ 08018

Dear Mr. Clark:

In May I will be receiving my M.B.A. degree from Temple University. While a great many firms will be coming to campus, my capabilities go beyond the routine type of training positions that most of these recruiters offer.

I have held a part-time supervisory position at Eastern National Bank for the past two years. When combined with my three years of military experience as a platoon leader in the Marine Corps, I believe I am far more prepared than the usual graduate to deal with the most demanding of business problems.

I am enclosing a resume. There is, of course, much about my conceptual and management abilities that cannot be reflected in print. An interview would reveal them. I will call you next week to discuss a convenient time for meeting.

Sincerely,

John Ramrod

Enc.

Gerald Scott
0000 Meadows Lane
Fresh Meadows, NY 11365
(718) 555-5555 - Residence

August 14, 1998

Mr. Ivan Milton, Chief of Staff
Boston Parks Department
830 Sixth Avenue
Boston, MA 10358

Dear Mr. Milton:

Ms. Joan Ridley informed me yesterday of an employment opportunity for a forester in the Street Tree Planting Division. As a native Bostonian and a practicing consultant forester in Boston with six years of experience, I thought you and I should discuss this position.

If you do not have a current need, please pass my resume along to someone who is looking for an efficient, budget-conscious, and knowledgeable forester.

Thank you!

Sincerely,

Gerald Scott

Enc.: Resume

Carl Langley
116 Fox Road
Springfield, PA 19064
(610) 555-1456


November 7, 1998


Kyle Wright
Wrights Brothers
1033 Saint Mary Avenue
Longwood, PA 20087

Dear Mr. Kyle Wright:

While exploring the Web last night, I discovered your job listing for a Professional Fund Raiser.

The position sounds ideal for me, as I have extensive experience in the areas required: revitalizing donor relations, recruiting influential personalities and officials, designing motivational marketing materials, and creating a stronger corporate image and greater positive awareness.

- For Hope International, I increased total donations from $86 million to $135 million.

- At Humanitarian America, I recruited more than 200 distinguished Americans, leading to an increase in donations of $3.9 million in the first year.

As the enclosed resume indicates, my track record in donor relations speaks for itself. And, needless to say, my extensive contacts with top executives, entertainers, and members of Congress are vital for managing productive fund-raising efforts.

I'll call your office next week to arrange a personal meeting with you. Until then, I ask that you keep this application confidential. Thank you.

Sincerely yours,


Carl Langley

Enc.

HELEN MARTINEZ
116 Wolf Street
Springfield, PA 19064
(610) 555-0110

September 13, 1998

Ms. Karen Lockwood
Robson Mechanics, Inc.
167 Ridgemore Avenue
Maryview, NJ

Dear Ms. Lockwood:

Are you interested in an executive who would immediately contribute to your company's profitability?

My experience in general management and new business development has allowed me to achieve a number of notable accomplishments, including the following:

- Reversed four years of losses, achieving sales of $124M with $9.5M in profit within three years.
- Achieved #2 market share and increased sales by $29M within 18 months.
- Grew consumer products division from $3.2M to $9.6M in the first year and $28.2M in the second year.

If you have a need for someone on your management team with my qualifications, please call me.

Sincerely,

Helen Martinez

Enc.

Cheryl Smith
11-11 James Street
New York, NY 11223
(212) 000-0000

October 29, 1998

Anna M. Sassoon, Director of Human Resources
City Hospital/Island Correctional Facility
101 Boylston Street
Boston, MA 10457

Dear Ms. Sassoon:

During my employment with Mount Evans Medical Center, I became knowledgeable and experienced in prison health services.

I offer my years of experience at St. John's Mental Health Ward (C-71) as well as extensive pharmacy experiences elsewhere.

I am organized, efficient and well-trained—all qualities that would prove to be assets to your organization. Also, I am skilled at working with corrections officials, and with professionals within many disciplines.

Let's speak soon!

Sincerely,

Cheryl Smith

Enc.: Resume

Ellen Munson
1234 Lincoln Street
Tiffin, OH  44883
(419) 555-5555


July 9, 1998


Mr. John Dow, Principal
Peterson High School
Indianapolis, IN 46200

Dear Mr. Dow:

Are you looking for a globally experienced teacher with significant skills in computer instruction and administration?

Mel Johnson suggested that I enclose my resume to your attention. I received my certification from NYS in September '93 and have taught for several years in both New York and India, using hands-on techniques and technology.  I possess superior computer knowledge (CBL programs such as geometers sketchpad, mathematica), leadership and organizational skills, and I am capable of working independently or as a team member in an educational or administrative environment.

I believe that my diverse background and my qualifications would make me an outstanding asset to your school.  I would welcome a personal interview to discuss in detail my ability as a teacher and my compatibility with the rest of your staff.

Sincerely,



Ellen Munson

Enc.:  Resume

Eileen M. Vantage
00-00 Elmhurst Avenue
Boston, MA 11373
(617) 000-0000


January 13, 1999


Mel Alfree
ABC Healthcare Corporation
123 Main Street
Boston, MA 02121

Dear Mr. Alfree:

As a recent graduate from Boston College - Continuing Education Program with a Certificate in Physician and Hospital Billing, I noted your opening for billing specialists with interest.

My coursework was praised by my instructor as "exemplary," and I received excellent grades in my courses on the VanTak invoicing system, which I understand your organization uses.

I am quick to grasp new and complex situations, providing consistent and timely responses. I feel that with my background and the challenges facing your organization, an excellent opportunity for me to help you streamline your billing procedures exists.

Let's meet soon!

Sincerely,


Eileen M. Vantage

Enclosure

JOHN PAPPAS
70 Steven Lane
Cedar Brook, NJ 08018
(609) 555-1234


February 8, 1999


Herb Ridgemore, Vice President
ABC Company
2087 4th Street
Cedarside, NJ 09188

Dear Mr. Ridgemore:

If you are looking for a Human Resource executive with strong leadership abilities who:

- is accustomed to a rapidly changing, entrepreneurial type growth environment,
- can help develop a corporate culture that supports quality management and self-directed work teams, and
- understands ROI accountability for HR issues and has a bottom-line orientation,

please give me a call. I am confident that I can make an immediate contribution to the improved management of your company's human resources.

I look forward to hearing from you.

Sincerely yours,


John Pappas

Enc.

Carol Jones
55555 Worth Street
New York, NY 55555
(555) 555-5555

October 20, 1998

Rich Bielawski, Vice President, Human Resources
St. Joan's Hospital
20-20 183rd Street
New York, NY 11111

Dear Mr. Bielawski:

Thanks for taking the time to discuss your search for an Intensive Care Nurse. As you requested, I'm enclosing my resume.

My most recent personnel evaluation reads: "The consistent, efficient manner in which you accept responsibility, pursue assignments and achieve all objectives has made you an extremely valuable member of this medical team. Your performance has been excellent."

I would welcome the opportunity for an interview to further discuss the position. Thank you for your consideration.

Sincerely,

Carol Jones

Enclosure

**Lila Peter, M.D.**
**00-00 3rd Street**
**White Plains, New York 11355**
**(718) 000-0000**

October 13, 1998

Dr. Samuel Wallace
Besserton Medical Center
One Besserton Place
Besserton, NY 11355

Dear Dr. Wallace:

Thanks for asking for a look at my resume during our phone call today.

As I mentioned, I am ABIM certified in Internal Medicine, and will complete my pulmonary fellowship in June 1999 from Stoneway Hospital Center in Stoneway, New York.

I am looking forward to hearing from you.

Sincerely yours,

Lila Peter

Enc.

**Jennifer May**
**00-000 Bell Boulevard**
**Bayville, New York 11777**
**(555) 555-5555**

January 6, 1999

John Vinson
Empire Financial Group
345 Mentor Avenue
Bayville, NY 11777

Dear Mr. Vinson:

If you are looking for someone who has a record of proven experience as a loan officer, and who had demonstrated competency in successfully administering highly profitable business loans of $500,000 and over, we should schedule an interview.

I look forward to speaking with you soon!

Sincerely,

Jennifer May

Enclosure

Claire Nastrom
13 Lincoln Avenue
Miami, FL 01176
(305) 555-5555

March 8, 1999

Lisa Lewiston
Rocker Industries
1009 Washington Avenue
Miami, FL 01176

Dear Ms. Lewiston:

I was able to help my company reduce down time by more than 30% in just nine months. If you're interested in talking to someone who can deliver the same kinds of results to your firm, perhaps we should meet.

Please let me know if the enclosed resume is of interest to you.

Sincerely,

Claire Nastrom

Enc.

**Sally Oliveria**
**319 Smith Road**
**Nashua, NH 06000**
**(603) 555-5556**
**(603) 555-5557**

November 20, 1998

Northeast Cable Associates
Attention: Molly Franco
220 South Main
Nashua, NH 06001

Dear Ms. Franco:

Are you looking for a high achiever for your management trainee program?

Besides maintaining a 3.7 grade point average throughout high school and college, I earned the BFLA Entrepeneurship Award, the Basic Business Award, was named District Parliamentarian, and won 1st Place in the State Parliamentary Procedure Awards. I also made the Dean's list at Three Rivers Community College, and earned 2 scholarships.

Attached is my resume which outlines some of my other qualifications. May we meet to discuss further the contributions I could make to Universal Cablevision? You may call me at (603) 555-5556 during the day or (603) 555-5557 during evening hours.

Sincerely,

Sally Oliveria

Enc.

LAURA GUTHRIE
116 Fox Road
Springfield, PA 19064
(610) 322-1456


January 23, 1999

David Dorman
Lewiston International
197 East 3rd Street
New York, NY 11208

Dear Mr. Dorman:

Since graduating college I have been acquiring a depth of knowledge in sales and marketing, achieving my current position of Marketing Director approximately five years ago.

In the course of this experience I have developed a solid foundation in sales and marketing, sales promotion, budgeting, forecasting, presentations, new product planning and market research. This background has been acquired in the course of 13 years with three major producers of high-tech telecommunications products.

This leads me to what I can offer you. Just as I helped lead my current company from a $2.5 million loss to a $3.7 million profit, I can utilize the same expertise to significantly improve your profitability and competitiveness in the marketplace. I've done it before and I can do it again— for you!

Because there's so much more to relate, I'd appreciate the opportunity for a personal meeting. I'm confident it could be both interesting and mutually profitable. May I hear from you?

Yours truly,


Laura Guthrie

Enc.

**Mary Warren**
539 Spratwell Drive
Chicago, IL 60609
Home: (555) 555-1555   Office: (555) 555-5555

November 7, 1998

Mr. Richard R. Rickers, III, President
QualiCo, Inc.
55 Albrecht Drive
Lakeside, IL 60044

Dear Mr. Rickers:

Could your company be more profitable?  I can help as an innovative executive.

My management, sales, marketing, strategic planning and business development experience has produced the following results:

- Doubled revenue (from $50 million to $100 million) in 12 months.
- Saved $2 million annually by restructuring sales organization.

If you have a need, I will do an excellent job for you.

Sincerely,

Mary Warren

Enc.

Stephanie Brown
111-11 10th Road
Flushing, NY 11354
(718) 000-0000

February 6, 1999

Ms. Sarah Turner
Ridley Mechanics, Human Resources
555 West 63rd Street, 14th Floor
Chicago, IL 10019

Dear Ms. Turner:

Thanks for discussing employment opportunities with me today! As you requested, I'm enclosing my resume.

If you're interested in working with a mechanical engineer whose work in system design and cost estimates was praised by a Fortune 500 client as "the strongest we have ever seen," we should meet in person.

I am a responsible, conscientious employee who works well alone or in a group. I am organized, efficient and well-trained. Here's hoping we can get together soon!

Sincerely,

Stephanie Brown

Enclosure

Jenny Jones
5555 West End Avenue
New York, NY 55555
(212) 000-0000

September 15, 1998

Director of Human Resources
Johnson Medical Center
One Hospital Plaza
New York, NY  55555

Dear Sir/Madam:

In reference to your posted opening for a medical assistant—are you interested in speaking with someone who offers two years of experience, three consecutive "excellent" evaluations on quarterly salary reviews, and a proven record of commitment to the highest quality care?

I hope we can speak soon.

Sincerely,

Jenny Jones

Enc.

Lou Rodriguez
409 Sycamore Lane
New York, NY 11209
(212) 555-5555


March 7, 1999


John Markle
Lewiston Incorporated
167 Main Street
Brooklyn, NY 11202

Dear Mr. Markle:

If my research is correct, you're interested in expanding into the southeastern market.

Would you be interested in speaking with an accomplished sales management professional more than 16 years of experience in medical instrument sales in the southeast? In my current position, I've been able to:

- Develop three of my company's past seven national "Most Valuable Player" recipients.
- Help increase our average dollar volume per sale by 27% during my tenure.
- Train and motivate a sales staff of sixteen.

If the attached resume is not of interest to you, may I ask that you forward it to someone who would benefit from what I have to offer?

Sincerely,


Lou Rodriguez

Enclosure

Lorraine Moore
55-55 99th Street
Jackson Heights, NY 11372
(718) 555-5555

March 22, 1999

Melanie Stopweather
Journey Halfway House
333 Main Street
Brenton, NY 11366

Dear Ms. Stopweather:

If you're looking for a mental health professional with seven years of experience in providing care to troubled adolescents, we should talk.

My abilities, professionalism and sense of caring enable me to work with a variety of individuals, both in a group as well as on a one-to-one basis. My dedication to the emotional well-being of my patients has led to three citations for innovation and excellence at Crestcare Facilities, my current employer.

I look forward to hearing from you in the very near future.

Very truly yours,

Lorraine Moore, C.S.W.

Enclosure

SHARON LEVINE
23 Dorothy Drive
Springfield, PA 19064
(610) 322-1456

May 27, 1999

Mr. Lewis Long
Long Sayles & Co., Inc.
558 Drewmore Avenue
Peterson, PA 11983

Dear Mr. Long:

My research indicates that your firm specializes in executive searches in the financial industry. Among your clients you may have one that is seeking a Mortgage Banking Officer with strong leadership abilities and a record of running efficient and profitable loan operations.

My technical expertise includes:

- Conventional, VA, FHA, FHLMC, FNMA, prime/subprime markets, retention, and credit risk scoring.
- Loan processing, closing, and underwriting with retail, broker, wholesale and conduit operations.

I am open to location, dependent upon the specifics of the opportunity. My salary requirements are in the $70,000 to $80,000 range.

As a follow-up to this correspondence, I will call you next week to determine what opportunities may exist with your clients. If no appropriate opportunities exist, I would welcome your ideas and counsel.

Sincerely yours,

Sharon Levine

Enc.

Hannah Drummond
000-00 18th Avenue
Bronx, NY 10455
(718) 000-0000


August 1, 1998


Martin Jones
Veritop Corporation
345 Elm Street
New York, NY 10106

Dear Mr. Jones:

　　Are you interested in meeting with an operations professional who reduced the average lag between customer order and shipping date by 31% during her first six months on the job?

　　If so, we should meet to discuss ways that I can contribute to your organization's operational effectiveness and increase profitability.

　　I am enclosing a copy of my resume for your review. I look forward to hearing from you at your earliest possible convenience and hope we can schedule a personal interview.

Sincerely yours,


Hannah Drummond

Enclosure

Beverly Peterson, R.N.
5555 50th Street
Flushing, NY 11357
(212) 555-1212

March 16, 1999

Ms. Lila Motley
Lewis Park School
123 West 57th Street
New York, NY 10125

Dear Ms. Motley:

Let me know if you need an experienced pediatric intensive care nurse.

I have been working as a pediatric intensive care nurse at Winfred University Hospital in Vine, New York for more than one year. I have extensive experience in caring for pediatric patients with complex medical conditions. I am interested in expanding my professional experience to include caring for children with special needs outside the acute care, hospital setting. As a pediatric nurse, I have a deep love and compassion in caring for children.

I am a highly motivated and energetic individual and am eager to become a contributing member to your institution. I also have a working knowledge of Spanish, especially in medical terminology.

Thank you for your consideration.

Sincerely,

Beverly Peterson, R.N.

Enclosure

Robert Robertson
55-55 55th Street
Dix Hills, NY 10055
(555) 555-5555

December 23, 1998

Johnson's
21 Johnson Plaza
Highside, NY 11735

Attention:  Ms. Katherine Jones, Director of Personnel
Fax No.:    (516) 293-1451

Objective:  Wine Manager Position Career

Dear Ms. Jones:

Our mutual acquaintance Robert Sindley suggested that I pass along my resume in reference to the above position.

Bob is a subscriber to my monthly newsletter, "GLOBAL WINE NEWS," which has a circulation of several thousand devoted readers, but which I am in the process of selling.

I'm looking forward to hearing from you soon so that we may set up a personal interview.

Sincerely,

Robert Robertson

Enc.

Christine James, RPH
5125 Amy Street
Brooklyn, NY 11111
(718) 555-3333


November 24, 1998


Stan Marano
Rivers University Hospital, Human Resources
2245 East Drive
New York, NY 11755

Dear Mr. Marano:

Thanks for taking the time to speak to me today about your opening for a hospital pharmacist.

I am Registered Pharmacist in New York with extensive experience in retail pharmacy. I have also had six months of experience as a volunteer intern at Hospital Medical Center. Melanie George, my supervisor, described my work as "outstanding" and has written that I would "make an excellent addition to any hospital staff."

Let's speak soon!

Sincerely,


Christine James, RPH

Enc.

Louise Partridge
23 West 17th Street
New York, NY 11208
(212) 555-5555


March 3, 1999


Mr. Richard Rivers
Green Magazine
287 West 55th Street
New York, NY 11304

Dear Mr. Rivers:

   Maria Thomas mentioned that you were on the lookout for news photographers. If your organization is interested in connecting with an experienced photojournalist who's won the Ryan Bode Award for excellence in photographic essays in the Chicago area, we should speak.

   My resume is enclosed; I think it would benefit both of us to meet and review my portfolio. If you agree, please give me a call.

Sincerely,


Louise Partridge

Enc.

John Park
209 Atlantic Avenue
Brooklyn, NY 11204
(718) 555-5555


February 2, 1999


Ms. Mary Stanley
Sky Airlines
1209 4th Street
Brooklyn, NY 11201

Dear Ms. Stanley:

Having recently concluded a six-year stint in the Air Force, I read about your airline's plans for expansion (*Aviation Journal,* January 25, 1998) with some interest.

If your organization is interested in speaking with a former test pilot with 2200 hours of high-performance fighter time, significant experience in air shows, and a spotless safety record, we should talk. I'm enclosing my resume; I look forward to speaking with you soon.

Sincerely,


John Park

Enc.

**MARTIN L. BROWN**
580 West Beach Boulevard, 5-C
Short Beach, MS 39560
Home: (555) 555-5555

November 8, 1998

Mr. William T. Rose, Chief Executive Officer
Roosevelt Lumber & Cedar Company
1340 Streatham Way
Cambridge, MA 02139

Dear Mr. Rose:

If you know anyone who could use a senior-level plant/project manager with large plant turnaround experience, please pass my resume on to them or call me.

Sincerely yours,

Martin L. Brown

Enc.

Mary Lewiston
75 Lakeview Street
Evanston, IL 60606
(313) 555-6787

August 10, 1998

Mr. Frank Everight, Vice President
Local Communications
156 7th Avenue
Chicago, IL 60606

Dear Mr. Everight:

I understand from your recent "Public Broadcasting Profile" in *Airwaves* that one of your station's key objectives for the coming five years is to develop more programming intended for a national public television audience.

I was the producer of the documentary "Children of the Night: Boston's Young and Homeless," which was taken on for national broadcast as part of the *Viewpoint* series. The program won a network award for Best Original Documentary at the regional New England Public Broadcasting Convention.

The recent online posting for a Staff Producer at WHCI caught my eye. Perhaps we could meet to discuss it in person?

Sincerely,


Mary Lewiston


P.S.: I will call your office on Tuesday morning, August 13, to discuss this opportunity further.

Michael Thompson
111-11 111th Street
Cambria Heights, NY 11111
(718) 555-5555


September 28, 1998


Ray Tyler
VV Productions
222 East 98th Street, 4th Floor
New York, NY 10017

Dear Mr. Tyler:

Thanks for speaking with me yesterday about your opening for a production assistant.

As I mentioned, I have experience working as production design PA for four weeks at Vera Productions where I decorated the set, purchased props, and maintained continuity throughout the production. My work was praised by the head of Vera as "absolutely superb."

You asked for a copy of my resume; that's enclosed. I hope to hear from you in the near future.

Thank you for your consideration!

Sincerely,


Michael Thompson

Enc.

Avery Copeland
6010 North College Avenue
Cedar Brook, NJ 08018
(609) 975-5429


January 27, 1999


Sarah Johnson
Johnson Sales
209 7th Street
Bayside, NJ 20089

Dear Ms. Johnson:

Directing major construction projects and managing existing properties is my expertise. I am a Project and Facilities Manager who:
- has developed nearly $70 million in new construction over the past eight years,
- manages more than 3.2 million sq. ft. of commercial and industrial property, and
- is accustomed to effectively dealing with owners, investors, subcontractors, architects, bankers, inspectors, buyers, and other interested parties.

If you have a need for someone on your management team who can manage multiple projects more efficiently and profitably, please give me a call.

Your consideration is much appreciated.

Sincerely yours,


Avery Copeland

Enc.

William Lowe
55 Lauren Road
New York, NY 11111
(555) 555-0000

January 19, 1999

Lilly O'Brien, Personnel Manager
Proofreaders Personnel
100 Ninth Avenue, Suite 501
New York, NY 10011

Dear Ms. O'Brien:

I spoke on the telephone today with Mel James in your office regarding employment possibilities, and he suggested that I send you a copy of my resume.

I have taken a course in legal proofreading, and I also have experience in financial proofreading. I have excellent English skills—I taught English abroad for several years—and I can proofread material in French, if the need for that arises.

Thank you very much for your consideration.

Sincerely yours,

William Lowe

Enc.

**DENISE E. TOULON**
2120 Westmoreland Street
Ridgemore, MA 11363
(718) 555-0000

February 13, 1999

Dr. Katherine Morely, Assistant Commissioner
Boston Department of Health
Bureau of Environmental Sciences
125 Worth Street
Boston, MA 02113

Dear Dr. Morely:

Are you interested in speaking with an applicant who has amassed 16 years of extensive and progressive experience with the Boston Board of Education's, Office of School Food and Nutrition Services (OSFNS) and is thoroughly versed in all aspects of operations and delivery systems?

I am considered an exceptional leader and persuasive communicator and presenter who is attentive to detail without losing sight of overall goals. Additionally, I am an effective problem-solver who is viewed as a team player, strong in communication skills with a full appreciation of compliance issues, food safety and the nutritional well-being of our children.

I am confident that I can be of particular value to the Department of Health and am most appreciative of the opportunity to further discuss my qualifications and experience with you.

Thank you for your consideration, I can be reached as indicated above.

Sincerely,


Denise E. Toulon

Enc.

Martin Chen
23 Lakewood Drive
San Francisco, CA 94109
(415) 555-5555


July 13, 1998


Lewis Stanford, II
Stanford & Sons, Inc.
3445 Financial Way
San Francisco, CA 94109

Dear Mr. Stanford:

Mark Ryan informed me that, given your organization's recent decision to enter the publishing field, you're in need of a qualified professional to support publicity campaigns. If that's the case, we should speak!

I'm enclosing my resume—as you'll see, one if its highlights was my work on the Glamour-Way project. Over a period of six weeks, I booked our firm's Vice President of Marketing on more than 100 local and national broadcast stations, and secured more than 75 positive print mentions and feature articles.

Does this record of accomplishment match up with your current objectives?

Sincerely,


Martin Chen

Enc.

P.S.: I will plan on calling your office on Monday morning, July 16, to speak about this opportunity further.

Julia Sheldon
19-14 Fifth Street
Springfield, PA 19064
(610) 555-1456


September 25, 1998

Mr. Riley Lewiston
Spence Agency
204 60th Street
Clearview, PA 20889

Dear Mr. Lewiston:

As an award-winning Public Relations Officer with strengths in media relations, stockholder relations, employee communications and public/community relations, please consider the strengths I would bring to your organization.

- Develop strategy and direct the ongoing communications effort with stockholders, the media, employees, and the general public.
- Produce quarterly/annual reports for stockholders and manage the annual stockholders meeting.
- Write all press releases, handle national media inquiries, and serve as the company spokesperson with the financial and trade media.
- Write all major speeches and provide communications counsel to senior executives and the Board of Directors.

I am prepared to handle the most challenging of assignments and would appreciate the opportunity to discuss in more detail the valuable contributions I would bring to your firm. If you have a need for someone with my qualifications, I can be reached at 610-555-1456.

Sincerely yours,


Julia Sheldon

Enc.

**MICHELLE SPENCER**
00-00 Forest Avenue
Corona, New York 11368
(718) 555-5555

September 27, 1998

Marvin Paulsen
Pierceway Technologies
1616 Edison Avenue
Brentwood, NY 11111

Dear Mr. Paulsen:

If you are interested in meeting with a quality control inspector with a 14-year record of achievement at one of the nation's most prestigious engineering organizations, we should get together. I can promise a high level of efficiency, enthusiasm and vigor applied to any assignments given.

My resume is enclosed. An opportunity to meet with you personally would be a privilege and a pleasure.

I look forward to your reply.

Sincerely,

Michelle Spencer

Enc. Resume

**MICHAEL BROWN**
**800 Elm Street**
**Clearview, CA 90009**
**(555) 555-5555**

October 25, 1998

Mark Morrison
Vice President of Manufacturing & Paris Operations
More Foods, Inc.
P.O. Box 9016
Paris, TX 75461-9016

Dear Mr. Morrison:

If you know someone who could use an executive experienced in sales and marketing management who:

- attained #2 ranking out of 42 regions,
- achieved 153% of quota, and
- revitalized a poorly performing district, increasing sales from $12 million to $66 million in 1 year,

please pass my resume on to that individual or call me.

Thank you.

Sincerely yours,


Michael Brown

Enc.

Beatrice Jones
50-57 Beech Street
Los Angeles, CA 90068
(213) 555-5555

November 19, 1998

JoEllen Garcia
Dwayne Associates
111 8th Street
Santa Monica, CA 90405

Dear Ms. Garcia:

Are you interested in speaking to a registered nurses/supervisor who was cited for "superior care and administrative ability" in her most recent salary review?

My background includes practical experience in staff supervision, psychiatry, geriatric, medical and surgical nursing. I am experienced in M.D.S., comprehensive care planning and PRI. I am a good communicator, well-organized, assertive and eager to learn. I am confident that I will be an asset to your organization.

Please contact me so that we may discuss how my job qualifications may fulfill your requirements.

Sincerely,


Beatrice Jones

Enc.: Resume

Ryan Marquez
122 Clearview Drive
Palmetto, CA 11903
(306) 555-5555

February 17, 1999

Ms. Cathryn Cruise, Editor-in-Chief
Palmetto Times
1098 Bluffview Boulevard
Palmetto, CA 11902

Dear Ms. Cruise:

Glenn Smith, in your communications office, mentioned that your local news department was expanding. If your organization is interested in the services of a dedicated, detail-oriented reporter with seven local reporting awards to his credit, we should meet.

As your office suggested, I'm enclosing my resume. Is it of interest to you or someone else in your organization?

Sincerely,

Ryan Marquez

Enc.

Jane Macasia
55-55 Forest Avenue
Ridgewood, NY 11385
(718) 555-5555


September 11, 1998


Dr. Welton James
Bensonville Hospital
111 Main Street
Bensonville, NY 11399

Dear Dr. James:

Are you interested in working with a highly qualified, internationally experienced medical professional?

A native of the Philippines, I passed USMLE step I in June 1997 with a score in the top 3 percent, and I took USMLE step II in August 1998.

I am enclosing my application for a position as a PGY I resident in your program, as well as my resume. I look forward to receiving your reply.

Yours cordially,


Jane Macasia

Enclosure

September 11, 1998

**From:** **Carlotta Schwab**
**To:** **Dr. Harvey Wilson**
**Subject:** **Application Seeking a PGY-1 Position in the Session Starting January 1999 or July 1999**

Dear Dr. Wilson:

It gives me immense pleasure to apply to your residency program. My application and resume are enclosed.

I hold a solid ECFMG Certificate, a M.P.H. from the University of Connecticut (where I was awarded a Pacific Fellowship by the American Association of University Women for Graduate Study, due to my 4.0 G.P.A.). I have passed both the USMLE and FMGEMS and I have current ACLS Certification. I am a permanent resident in the U.S.

With a view to pursuing my ultimate goal of becoming a primary care physician, I aim to obtain my residency training in an excellent institution with high academic standards. I am looking forward to our future association and I am convinced that, if I am able to work as a member of your medical team, I will be a productive team member.

Thank you in advance for your consideration.

Sincerely,

Carlotta Schwab

Enc.

**RAYMOND SEMA**
**18 Hatcher Lane**
**Spicewood, TX 78669**
**(609) 975-5429**

January 27, 1999

Thea Johnson
Johnson Sales
108 77th Avenue
Austin, TX 78722

Dear Ms. Johnson:

Henry Ford once said, "Whether you think you can or think you can't—you are right." I think I can successfully fill your new National Sales Manager vacancy!

As a District Sales Manager, I set up a branch office that increased sales and profits by 26% and 57% respectively, in the first year of operation. I then moved into a larger territory and reversed a $480,000 annual losing trend into a $237,000 profit.

I think I could do as well for you and I'd like to try. My immediate interest is in obtaining a regional sales manager's position that offers superior potential for someone who can prove his worth.

Attached is a resume which outlines some of my further qualifications. May we meet to discuss the contributions which I know I can make to your firm?

I look forward to hearing from you.

Sincerely,


Raymond Sema

Enc.

Elaine Jones
343 Del Mar Drive
Indianapolis, IN 46260
(317) 555-5555

January 4, 1999

Les Katz
ABC Corporation
167 Main Street
Indianapolis, IN 46202

Dear Mr. Katz:

Gene Farley, of Optimark, suggested I contact you; he said you were trying to find ways to bring your sales staff's performance to the next level.

Can you use a seasoned district sales manager who increased revenue for nine consecutive quarters? If so, we should talk. If not, I'd appreciate it if you'd pass along the enclosed resume to someone who might benefit from my experience.

Sincerely,

Elaine Jones

Enclosure: Resume

JAMES R. ESFORMES
18 Hatcher Lane
Schaumberg, IL 60195
(708) 555-1222

October 23, 1998

Susan Fuzia
ABC Sales
233 Bay Street
Chicago, IL 60652

Dear Ms. Fuzia:

My expertise is spearheading dynamic sales and market share growth. As the Regional Sales Manager of a $13.5 million territory, some of my accomplishments include:

- Doubled prospect client presentations, leading to a 63% increase in sales over a 1 year period.
- Devised a plan to utilize obsolete inventory items, generating $1.1 million in revenues.
- Achieved 115%, 138%, and 156% of quota during the last three consecutive years.

The ability to manage the continued growth of both national and local accounts is a strength that would allow me to make a significant contribution to your firm's profitability and competitiveness.

I will call you early next week to see when we can meet to discuss how I might help you achieve record sales in the coming years. In the interim, I am enclosing my resume for your review. Thank you for your time and consideration.

Sincerely yours,

James R. Esformes

Enc.

**JOHN FARKAS**
21 Countrybrook Lane
Cedar Brook, NJ 08018
(609) 555-5429

September 19, 1998

Ms. Stephanie Mears, Vice President
Clear Dimensions
117 Sycamore Street
Hackensack, NJ 11903

Dear Ms. Mears:

Could you use a goal-oriented sales representative who took a territory from less than $500,000 in sales to more than $2 million over an 18-month period?

Several of my accomplishments include:
- Opened 76 accounts in the first year with sales in excess of $1.25 million.
- Recipient of three "Platinum Key" sales awards for three consecutive years.
- Revitalized stagnate product and achieved 34% of market share within a two-year period.

If you have a need for the same types of results, please contact me at (609) 555-5429 so that we might discuss the contributions I could make as part of your team.

Your time and consideration is most appreciated.

Sincerely yours,

John Farkas

Enc.

Aaron Gruber
3 Bayside Drive
San Francisco, CA 94109
(415) 555-5555

July 24, 1999

Mr. Mark Acton
Acton Corporation
1034 Route 3
San Francisco, CA 94109

Dear Mr. Acton:

As a salesperson for Jumbo Widget, I've exceeded quota 19 out of a possible 23 quarters, and been named my organization's Most Valuable Player of the Year three times.

If you're looking for a salesperson with significant experience in retail and wholesale widget environments, we should talk!

Sincerely,

Aaron Gruber

Enc.

Ellen Fry
337 East Riverside Drive
New York, NY 10020
(212) 555-3344

February 29, 1999

Ms. Rosa Rodriguez
Lewiston, Inc.
3378 Broadway
New York, NY 10017

Dear Ms. Rodriguez:

Do you know of anyone who would benefit from talking to a seasoned, experienced ad space salesperson who sold the highest square-inch total in the biggest ad-page issue in the publication's history?

If so, perhaps you could forward my resume. Many thanks!

Sincerely,

Ellen Fry

Enclosure

Martha Scher
203 Clearview Street
Seattle, WA 98040
(214) 555-5555


January 5, 1999


Ms. Stacey Everston
Everston Real Estate
1209 Atlantic Avenue
Seattle, WA 98045

Dear Ms. Everston:

Thanks for taking the time to speak with me about what you're looking for in a real estate salesperson. I think your goal of developing a client base that will yield $30 million in sales in your next fiscal year is eminently achievable.

At Overview Real Estate, I set a new company record for quarterly sales performance—$3.2 million in total billings—and I did it by setting up a new lead tracking system that has since been implemented companywide. I'd like to get together with you to discuss how I established this system—and how it might work in your organization.

As you requested, I'm sending along a copy of my resume. I look forward to speaking with you again soon!

Sincerely,


Martha Scher

Enclosure

Twyla McVey
77 Essex Street
Middleton, MA 01949
(555) 555-4627, ext. 302 (day)
(555) 555-6622 (evenings)

November 20, 1998

Box 919
Tri-Town Transcript
Danvers, MA 01972

To Whom It May Concern:

For the past 18 years, I have held several successful sales positions including; real estate sales 10 years (3 as a Broker); 5 years as a Tupperware Manager, winning several national awards, including Salesperson of the Year at Morris National Real Estate

My background also includes Christian book sales; Avon, and Amway sales. I am highly computer-literate.

As your advertisement requests, I am enclosing my resume. May we meet to discuss further the contributions I could make to your company? You may call me at the numbers above at any time.

Cordially Yours,


Twyla McVey

Enclosure

Patricia Thompson
842 1st Avenue
Elmhurst, NY 11373
(718 555-5555


April 10, 1999


Mike Jones
Industrial Tower
999 Organization
Elmhurst, NY 11373

Dear Mr. Jones:

Our mutual acquaintance, Rosalyn McGraw, suggested I contact you about your opening for an office associate.

Rosalyn thought my background in working with salespeople—I served as support person for an office of 18 sales reps at BestWay Manufacturing—would be of interest. She also thought I should mention that I was named "Support Star of the Year" at BestWay's national awards ceremony in 1998.

I look forward to speaking with you about this opening!

Sincerely,


Patricia Thompson

Enclosure

Sarah Hart
75 Side Drive
Denver, CO 80202
(303) 555-5555


March 22, 1999


Patricia Hoffman
Peterson & Co.
2 Main Street
Denver, CO 80202

Dear Ms. Hoffman:

As a senior advertising executive for Del Mar Worldwide Creative, I've launched many successful campaigns, including one for a major automobile manufacturer that helped to increase market share from 14% to 25% in one fiscal year.

My resume is enclosed—if it's not of interest to you, perhaps you could pass it along to someone who would be interested in speaking with a creative, innovative marketing professional.

Sincerely,


Sarah Hart

Enclosure

### MEL FARTHING
240 Eastham Drive
Scottsdale, AZ 85999
Home: (602) 555-5590     Mobile: (602)555-5277

March 1, 1999

Michael R. Hammons, Chief Executive Officer
Standard U.S.A., Inc.
1 Centennial Avenue
Drewside, NJ 08854

Dear Mr. Hammons:

If your company needs a senior-level executive with diverse experience in management and rapid growth who took a company from a $2 million loss to a $1.5 million profit, please give me a call.

I am available for consulting until I find the best long-term match. Consulting can also be a bridge that brings us together for a full-time position.

If you do not have a current need, please pass my resume on to someone who needs to double profits as I have repeatedly done.

Sincerely yours,


Mel Farthing

Enclosure

PETER J. WARREN
142 Princes Court, London, England
Phone: 011 55 5555
Fax: 011 55 5555
US Message Center:
Phone: (800) 555-5555, (913) 555-5555
Fax: (800) 555-5555, (913) 555-5555

March 29, 1999

Sarah Shore, Vice President
SRP International, Limited
666 Steamboat Road
Stamford, CT 06830

Dear Ms. Shore:

Let me know if you could use a multilingual senior executive who would immediately contribute to your company's profitability.

My international experience in management and business development has produced results including:

- Simultaneously built 2 companies increasing sales from $4 million to $30 million with $8.7 profit.
- $150 million sales with $13 million profit achieved in first year after merging 2 companies.

I am fluent in English, Dutch, German and proficient in French. For 20 years I have lived and/or worked throughout Europe, the United Kingdom, North America, South America and the former Soviet Union.

I look forward to hearing from you.

Thank you.

Sincerely yours,

Peter J. Warren

Enclosure

**Mark Steadman**
2225 Bayside Court, San Francisco CA 94901
(415) 555-9152

January 6, 1999

Leonard Simon
ABC Company
714 Poplar Avenue
Rochester, NY 11907

Dear Mr. Simon:

Spearheading dynamic revenue and market share growth is my expertise. As a Senior Marketing Executive with broad-based experience who:

- Took a new Fortune 200 division from $4 million to $75 million in 3 years,
- Reversed market share decline, increasing unit sales 19% to 500,000 in 1 year, and
- Achieved a 195% increase in corporate volunteers for a national nonprofit organization.

I am confident that I can make a significant contribution to your organization's profitability and competitiveness in the marketplace.

If you think you might have a need for someone on your management team with my qualifications, please give me a call. Thank you.

Sincerely,


Mark Steadman

Enclosure

BILL BABCOCK
6675 Binsbee Road
Sarasota, FL 44444
(555) 555-5555

April 23, 1999

Mr. Devin Brown, President
Brown Motor Corporation
1 Main Street
New York, NY 10011

Dear Mr. Brown:

As a Senior Manager experienced in logistics, maintenance and safety management who
effectively managed a logistics/supply work system with $1.5 million budget and $150
million inventory system, I am seeking a position that will utilize my comprehensive
operations management skills.

If you know someone who could use a manager with my experience, please pass my
resume on to that individual or call me.

Sincerely yours,

Bill Babcock

Enclosure

**Daniel Harrison**
**0000 20th Street, Apt. #1**
**Boston, MA 02111**

January 14, 1999

Jacqueline Howards
Cleaner Water Resources
1111 7th Avenue
Boston, MA 02111

Dear Ms. Howards:

My father, John Harrison, an employee of Cleaner Water Resources, notified me that C.W.R. was looking to fill the position of Senior Project Liaison Manager. I believe that my experience as a Resident Engineer for the City of New York would prove beneficial to a growing company such as United Water Resources.

I have been working for the Massachusetts Department of Environmental Protection for five years as a Resident Engineer. I am in the Emergency Reconstruction Unit, which is responsible for the repair and the redesign of existing sewers. I am the sole representative on the job site and therefore responsible for coordinating several aspects of the job. In addition to redesigning the sewer, I am also involved with the telephone, electric and gas companies. All of the utilities are involved in underground excavation in the city of Boston, and their concerns must be incorporated into the design scope of the project. This requires the skill of balancing the needs of the city with the interest of the utilities.

Because of the nature of the road construction, my ability to communicate has been finely tuned. Good communication skills are paramount in getting a job done according to schedule—and 89% of my projects over the past five years have been completed on or before established deadlines.

I have enclosed a copy of my resume, which gives you more specific information as to my background and accomplishments. I look forward to meeting with you and sharing ideas.

Many thanks for your time and consideration.

Sincerely,

Daniel T. Harrison

Enclosure

Ella Jones
343 Del Mar Drive
Boston, MA 02127
(617) 555-5555


August 14, 1998


Douglas Gilbert
Seismic Graphics Co., Inc.
187 Main Drive
Boston, MA 02127

Dear Mr. Gilbert:

Would you be interested in interviewing a senior technical writer with seven years of experience and 15 company or industry awards for excellence?

The documentation I established for our 1998 REWIND 6.0 release was praised for its "clarity, ease of access, accuracy of troubleshooting advice, and overall technical precision" by NEW RELEASE magazine. (January 1998.) If this is the type of approach you'd like to have in your next technical writing assignment, perhaps we could get together in person. If not, would you please pass along the enclosed resume to someone who would benefit from my experience?

Sincerely,


Ella Jones

Enclosure

Carolyn Smith, C.S.W.
714 Judge Street, Apt. 3C
Iowa City, IA 52333
(319) 555-5555


June 9, 1998


John Linn, C.S.W., Director of Social Work
Greenwich Hospital
6250 50th Street
Des Moines, IA 50266

Dear Mr. Linn:

Let me know if you're interested in meeting with a candidate who has seven years of experience as a hospital social worker and a proven record of personal crisis management in high-stress situations.

I would appreciate having the opportunity to discuss with you in person how I may be an asset to your department.

Thank you for your consideration

Sincerely,


Carolyn Smith, C.S.W.

Enclosure

Frank O. Schartz
P.O. Box 502345
Bayridge, NY 11294-1295
(212) 555-3547


August 2, 1998


Claudia Whitmore
Eckstein Brands, Inc.
422 East River Road
Cleveland, OH 44200

Dear Ms. Whitmore:

Don Riley suggested that I contact you and send along a copy of my resume for consideration for the position of Continuous Improvement Implementation Manager in your company.

I have been in the consulting business for more than 10 years and have had the opportunity of working with clients in small, medium and large companies both in the U.S. and Canada.

My expertise is in management systems, methods and process reengineering. Cost savings through improvements for clients have been considerable—in the $4 to $6 million range per project—and I hope to replicate these results in your organization if given the opportunity.

Thank you very much.

Sincerely,


Frank O. Schartz

Enclosure

**Mark Everest**
**34 Morgan Drive**
**Los Angeles, CA 90068**
**(818) 555-5555**

September 27, 1998

Janice Jackson
Jackson International
19547 Ventura Boulevard
Los Angeles, CA 90068

Dear Ms. Jackson:

Are you interested in meeting with a systems training specialist who helped to put together a training program that "significantly increased operational efficiency, and helped to increase productivity by at least 25%"?

That's what a past supervisor had to say about my performance during a recent personnel review. If you're looking for someone who can help you make complex computer systems accessible to everyone in your organization, we should get together.

Sincerely,

Mark Everest

Enclosure

Andrea Kraft
Route 1, Box 262
Sweet Cove, Virginia 24416 USA
Day (804) 555-2275
Evening (804) 555-9359

August 22, 1998

Maureen Allen
Joseph Technologies
53 Route 128
Ellis, Virginia 29047

Dear Ms. Allen:

I would like very much to discuss with you the contributions I could make to your company as part of your technical support staff.

I have been associated with the military for the past 21 years and have gained extensive experience in office automation and administration. In addition, I have taught several college computer courses and have become the unofficial computer specialist in our office. Some of my successes include:

- Provided an improved computerized layout that has since been adopted for all 66 Naval ROTC Units.
- Initiated the largest reorganization for the Squadron's 46 file cabinets of classified documents.
- Developed a computer suspense system that tracked and compiled critical statistical reports.

Attached is my resume, which outlines some of my other qualifications. May we meet to discuss further the contributions I could make to your company? You may call me at (804) 555-2275.

Cordially yours,

Andrea Kraft

Enc.

BENJAMIN KANE
116 Fox Road
Springfield, PA 19064
(610) 322-1456

July 23, 1998

Kathryn Haley
Bronson International
209 17th Street
New York, NY 11207

Dear Ms. Haley:

Travel is booming again in both the domestic and international market, and I have some ideas for helping my next employer to seize much of that business from the competition.

This statement may sound bold, but I am very serious. Please take a moment to consider some of my past accomplishments.

- Increased corporate clients by 300% resulting in $1.4 million in additional revenues.
- Reversed two years of losses in a regional office, generating $75,000 in profit in six months.
- Created a "Global Sales Program" that took a regional office from next to last to number three within two years (56 international offices).
- Led sales effort in new niche markets and secured incremental business, increasing market share by nearly 3%.

Travelers are spending dollars that could be going into your pocket. I can help remedy that situation. Of course, what my resume doesn't show is how well I'd fit into your team. To this end, I'll call your secretary next week to see when we might arrange a personal meeting.

Thank you.

Sincerely yours,

Benjamin Kane

Enc.

Louis Parker
727 33rd Avenue, Apt. 22
Brooks Hills, New York 11364
(718) 555-0000

July 3, 1998

S.A.I. Abbiategrasso
Corso Italia, 52
20100 Roma, Italia

Attn: John Bevilaqcua, Overseas Recruiter

Dear Mr. Bevilacqua:

Thanks for speaking with me today. I am currently seeking employment in Italy and have enclosed a copy of my most recent curriculum vitae for your review.

As you can see I possess a solid business background, most recently as a consultant in a banking environment and, previously, as manager of treasury operations with the American Securities Council. Reporting to the Council's treasurer, my responsibilities were diverse, including overseeing the daily operation of the billing and accounts receivable departments as well as handling various administrative functions. I am currently studying the Italian language and possess exceptional communication skills. My superior interpersonal qualities, together with a bachelor of science degree in finance, make me an ideal candidate for a position with a firm in Italy.

Your attention in this matter is greatly appreciated. I look forward to hearing from you.

Sincerely,

Louis Parker

Enclosure

Angela M. Cuomo
22 100th Place
East Elmhurst, NY 11369
(718) 555-5555


February 16, 1999


Mary Drummons, Nurse Recruiter
Wedgeworth V.A. Medical Center
405 East 49th Street
New York, NY 10010

Dear Ms. Drummons:

Thanks for taking to time to talk to me today about openings at Wedgeworth.

As an ex-marine, I honor and have great respect for this country's veterans and their families, and would offer a unique perspective on addressing their problems and concerns. I am currently enrolled in the nursing program at Brooklyn Community College. I will be graduating in June 1999 with an AAS in Nursing. I feel that I have good organizational and communication skills.

I would like to arrange for an interview at your convenience to further discuss my qualifications. Thank you for your time. I look forward to hearing from you soon.

Sincerely,



Angela M. Cuomo

Enc.: Resume

Pauline Ivers
1267 Riverside Drive
Austin, TX 78722
(512) 555-5555


March 26, 1999


Mr. Daniel Harrison
Harrison, Incorporated
12 West Hampton Drive
Austin, TX 78703

Dear Mr. Harrison:

Paul von Keppler wrote that "Optimists do not wait for improvement—they achieve it." I like to think I've taken that approach in developing superior, user-friendly web sites for my clients. The Dallas On-Line site I designed (www.dallasonline.com) now receives more than 30,000 hits weekly.

Your company newsletter suggests that you're looking for qualified, innovative web site designers. I'd like to talk about any full-time opportunities in this area you now have open. Please have a look at my resume, and give a call if you think, as I do, that there's the possibility of a good match.

Sincerely,


Pauline Ivers

Enc.

Robert Robertson
55-55 55th Street
Dix Hills, NY 10055
(555) 555-5555


December 23, 1998


Johnson's
21 Johnson Plaza
Highside, NY 11735

Attention:  Ms. Katherine Jones, Director of Personnel
Fax No.:    (516) 293-1451

Objective:  Wine Manager Position Career

Dear Ms. Jones:

Our mutual acquaintance Robert Sindley suggested that I pass along my resume in reference to the above position.

Bob is a subscriber to my monthly newsletter, "GLOBAL WINE NEWS," which has a circulation of several thousand devoted readers, but which I am in the process of selling.

I'm looking forward to hearing from you soon so that we may set up a personal interview.

Sincerely,


Robert Robertson

Enc.

# For Further Assistance

Included in the appendix for your convenience are: resources to help you further in your job search efforts; and two sample letter formats, illustrating a Talent Match letter and a follow-up thank-you note.

The resume and cover letter development firms listed in this appendix were instrumental in providing advice, guidance and sample cover letter templates. If you should need further help in developing attention-winning job search correspondence, you'll be doing yourself a favor if you give them a call.

Executive Resume
P.O. Box 79
Cedar Brook, NJ 08018-9998
(800) 563-6359

Executive Resume provides personal career-marketing services for professionals and executives seeking to advance or change their careers. Services range from the preparation of resumes and employment letters designed to optimize each client's marketability, to the custom design and management of an entire job-hunting campaign. These services may be utilized regardless of geographic location.

S&A Business Services, Inc.
615 North Prairie
P.O. Box 380
Bloomfield, MO 63825
(573) 568-4161

Provides professional assistance with resumes and cover letters for a wide variety of clients.

Resume Center of New York
15-23 120th Street
College Point, NY 11356
(718) 445-1956
(718) 445-1296 (fax)

Professional assistance on resumes, cover letters, personnel statements, business proposals, and other essential documents.

Resumes by James
102-30 Queens Boulevard
Forest Hills, NY 11375
(718) 896-6856
(718) 544-3300 (fax)

Serves the New York metropolitan area, and offers experience in resume and cover letter development in the following areas: health care, education, law enforcement, accounting, engineering, legal, air transport, military, sales, insurance, marketing, high-tech, customer service, hospitality industries, advertising, movies/television, and real estate.

WSA Corporation
11933 Johnson Drive
Shawnee, KS 66216-9905
(800) 972-2677

Since 1976, WSA has been helping executives, managers, and professionals with their career advancement. WSA's business is one of creating opportunity by introducing the right talent at the right time to the right companies. This is accomplished through the design of high-impact resumes and cover letters and their targeted distribution to the marketplace.

CAROL LONGLEY
116 Fox Road
Springfield, PA 19064
(610) 322-1456

March 9, 1999

Doris Richmond, Employment Manager
First National Bank
934 Main Street
Atlanta, GA 18374

Dear Ms. Richmond:

It appears that my qualifications are an excellent match for the position of *Manager of Employee Relations,* advertised in the Atlanta Business Chronicle.

| Your Requirements | My Qualifications |
|---|---|
| 5+ years of experience managing employee and corporate communication programs | 8 years of experience directing the ongoing communication effort with employees. |
| Experienced in preparing employee news-letters and other publications. | Write and distribute a bimonthly employee newsletter and other publications for 2,300 employees located at 16 locations |
| Familiar with a variety of multi-media techniques. | Use multi-media techniques such as closed circuit TV and satellite transmission. |
| Degree required, preferably in English. | B.A. and M.A. in English. Awarded Sigma Delta Chi (Outstanding Journalism Graduate). |

My resume is enclosed and I would welcome the opportunity to meet with you personally. Thank you for your consideration.

Sincerely,


Carol Longley

Enc.

CAROL LONGLEY
116 Fox Road
Springfield, PA 19064
(610) 322-1456


March 9, 1999

Doris Richmond, Employment Manager
First National Bank
934 Main Street
Atlanta, GA 18374

Dear Ms. Richmond:

Thanks so much for taking the time to fill me in on everything yesterday. I learned a great deal. I believe we can get that newsletter up and running within 30 days, as you hope to do!

There is a virtually perfect match here, and that's quite exciting. I'm eager to start work to help your department operate more smoothly, keep customers happy, and make your operational goals for this quarter a reality.

Once again, thanks for your time. I look forward to speaking with you soon.

Sincerely,


Carol Longley

# Index

Accounting, cover letter sample, 60
Achievements, 15, 38-39
Adaptability, success stories, 30
Administrative assistant, 22-23
  cover letter sample, 61
Advertising executive, cover letter
  sample, 134
Airplane pilot, cover letter sample,
  110
Anecdotes, for cover letter, 29
Animal care specialist, cover letter
  sample, 62
Annual reports, 23
Applications, 25
Art dealer, cover letter sample, 63
Avery, Michelle, 39

Billing specialist, cover letter
  sample, 64
Branch manager, cover letter
  sample, 65
Brand manager, cover letter
  sample, 66
Brevity,
  cover letter, 39
  importance of, 36

Change, success stories, 30
Chef, cover letter sample, 67
Chief of security, cover letter
  sample, 68
Civil engineer, cover letter sample,
  69
Clinical manager, cover letter
  sample, 70
Controller, cover letter sample, 71
Counselor, cover letter sample, 72

Cover letter,
  achievements, 38-39
  anecdotes, 29
  as highlighter, 34
  brevity, 36, 39
  creativity, 41-42
  customize, 36, 46
  design, 34-35
  don'ts, 35-36, 56
  expectations of, 33
  follow-up, 40-41
  mutual contacts, 38
  overused phrases, 36
  professionalism, 37
  purpose of, 33-34
  samples, 60-149
  success stories, 29-32
  third-party endorsements, 37-38
  too much copy, 36
  type size, 34
  use of "I", 36, 37
  with resume, 33-34
  within company, 20
Creativity,
  in cover letters, 41-42
  when to use, 42
Credit and collections manager,
  cover letter sample, 73
Customer orientation, success
  stories, 31
Customer service supervisor, cover
  letter sample, 74, 75
Customization, of cover letter, 36,
  46

Dedication, success stories, 31
Deputy superintendent, rapid
  transit, cover letter sample, 76

Design, 34
consistency, 35
matching paper, 34
templates, 34
type faces, 34
type size, 34
white space, 35
Desktop publishing specialist, cover
letter sample, 77
Distribution management, cover
letter sample, 78
Doctor, internal medicine specialist,
cover letter sample, 94
Doctor, resident, cover letter
sample, 123, 124
Driver, cover letter sample, 79
Driving instructor, cover letter
sample, 80

Economic trends, 23
Editor, cover letter sample, 81
Efficiency, success stories, 31
Engineering and development,
cover letter sample, 82
Environmental services engineer,
cover letter sample, 83
Executive Resume, 151
Executive,
international, cover letter
sample, 136
turnaround specialist, cover
letter sample, 135

Fashion designer, cover letter
sample, 84
Financial manager, cover letter
sample, 85
Follow-up letter, sample, 154
Forester, cover letter sample, 86
Formal job postings, 18
Fund raiser, cover letter sample, 87

General manager, cover letter
sample, 88
Goals, 15-16, 48

Gossip, 19

Health services specialist, cover
letter sample, 89
High school teacher, cover letter
sample, 90
Hiring supervisor, 22
"life story" letters, 36
radar screen, 18, 43
Hospital billing specialist, cover
letter sample, 91
Human resource professional, cover
letter sample, 92

Industry publications, 23
Industry trends, 24
Information-gathering, 22-24
Intensive care nurse, cover letter
sample, 93
Internal medicine specialist, cover
letter sample, 94
Interview, 51, 52

Job applications, 25
Job description, written, 22
Jobs,
at other companies, 21-24
number of replies to, 25
within company, 17-20

Leadership, success stories, 31-32
Library, research, 23-24
Loan office, cover letter sample, 95

Management information systems
specialist, cover letter sample,
96
Management trainee, cover letter
sample, 97
Marketing director, cover letter
sample, 98
Marketing executive, cover letter
sample, 99, 120, 137
Marketing, medical equipment,
cover letter sample, 102

Mechanical engineer, cover letter sample, 100

Medical assistant, cover letter sample, 101

Medical equipment sales, cover letter sample, 102

Medical resident, cover letter sample, 123, 124

Meetings, 43, 44

Mental health, cover letter sample, 103

Mission, 14

Mortgage banking officer, cover letter sample, 104

Nurse, cover letter sample, 93, 106, 121, 147

Operations manager, cover letter sample, 138

Operations specialist, cover letter sample, 105

Overused phrases, cover letter, 36

Paper,
    color, 34
    resume package, 34

Pediatric intensive care nurse, cover letter sample, 106

Periodicals, research, 23

Personnel manager, cover letter sample, 107

Pharmacist, cover letter sample, 108

Phone calls, 28
    follow-through, 41
    who initiates, 40

Phone interviews, avoiding, 44-45

Photographer, cover letter sample, 109

Pilot, cover letter sample, 110

Plant manager, cover letter sample, 111

Politics, within company, 17-20

Positive attitude, 47

President, assistant, 22

Producer, cover letter sample, 112

Production assistant, cover letter sample, 113

Profit orientation, success stories, 31

Project and facilities manager, cover letter sample, 114

Project liaison manager, cover letter sample, 139

Promotions, 15

Proofreader, cover letter sample, 115

Prove-it-to-me" question, 47

Public health administrator, cover letter sample, 116

Public relations associate, cover letter sample, 117

Public relations officer, cover letter sample, 118

Qualifications, of job, 18

Quality control specialist, cover letter sample, 119

Questions, 23, 47

Reference librarian, 23

Referral, 14

Regional marketing executive, cover letter sample, 120

Registered nurse, cover letter sample, 121

Rejection, 51-53

Reporter, cover letter sample, 122

Research, 22-24
    boss, 18-19
    importance of, 14
    job, 18-19
    library, 23-24
    on self, 14
    president's assistant, 23
    questions to ask, 19

Resume Center of New York, 152

Resume,
  delivering, 46
  design, 34
Resumes by James, 152
Rumors, 19

S&A Business Services, Inc., 151
Sales manager, cover letter sample,
  125, 126, 127
Sales support, cover letter sample,
  133
Sales, success stories, 31
Salesperson, cover letter sample,
  128, 129, 130, 131, 132
Senior advertising executive, cover
  letter sample, 134
Senior international executive,
  cover letter sample, 136
Senior marketing executive, cover
  letter sample, 137
Senior operations manager, cover
  letter sample, 138
Senior project liaison manager,
  cover letter sample, 139
Senior technical writer, cover letter
  sample, 140
Sense of purpose, 14
Skills, 15
Social worker, cover letter sample,
  141
Specific, 16
Success stories, 29-32, 48, 49
  adaptability, 30
  change, 30
  customer orientation, 31
  efficiency, 31
  leadership, 31-32
  profit orientation, 31
  talking to others, 32
  themes, 30-31
Systems expert, cover letter
  sample, 142
Systems training specialist, cover
  letter sample, 143

Talent Match letter, 24, 25-28, 44
  advantages, 28
  defined, 26
  groundwork, 29
  sample, 27, 153
Technical support person, cover
  letter sample, 144
Technical writer, cover letter
  sample, 140
Television producer, cover letter
  sample, 112
Text search retrieval computer, 23
Thank-you letter, sample, 154
Themes, success stories, 30-31
Third-party endorsements, 37-38
303 Off The Wall Ways to Get a
  Job, 41, 42
Trade magazines, 23, 24
Travel executive, cover letter
  sample, 145
Treasurer, cover letter sample, 146
Turnaround specialist, cover letter
  sample, 135
Type faces, 34
Type size, cover letter, 34

Veterans' center nursing specialist,
  cover letter sample, 147
Volunteer work, 15

Wall Street Journal, The, 24
Web site, 22
Web site designer, cover letter
  sample, 148
White space, 35
Wine manager, cover letter sample,
  149
Word-processing templates, 34
Work history, 29-30
Working with others, 15
WSA Corporation, 152